Emotional Intelligence at Work

Emotional Intelligence at Work

A Personal Operating System for Career Success

Richard M. Contino and Penelope J. Holt

BEP

BUSINESS EXPERT PRESS

Leader in applied, concise business books

Emotional Intelligence at Work:
A Personal Operating System for Career Success

Cover design by Charlene Kronstedt

Interior design by Exeter Premedia Services Private Ltd., Chennai, India

First published in 2021 by
Business Expert Press, LLC
222 East 46th Street, New York, NY 10017
www.businessexpertpress.com

ISBN-13: 978-1-63742-018-8 (paperback)
ISBN-13: 978-1-63742-019-5 (e-book)

Business Expert Press Business Career Development Collection

Collection ISSN: 2642-2123 (print)
Collection ISSN: 2642-2131 (electronic)

First edition: 2021

10 9 8 7 6 5 4 3 2 1

For Matt, May, and Sue

Description

Even though it is seldom acknowledged, the truth is that business runs on emotion—yours and almost everyone else's. And that emotion is often negative, leading us into bewilderment, dysfunction, and failure.

This book explains how to face up to this reality and respond by building street smarts and business emotional intelligence (BEQ). It supports your business success by developing your ability to recognize and effectively manage the destructive emotional tendencies, hidden agendas, and behaviors that exist all around you, and sometimes within you, that block business progress.

Emotions don't belong in the business process, we are told. And that's absolutely correct when destructive feelings disrupt the workplace. But here is the dirty little secret: Irrational and runaway feelings nevertheless dominate in many businesses *and hold back professionals who are crippled by emotional dynamics that often play out beyond conscious awareness and their control.*

Learn how and why emotions are a controlling factor in every career or business success and failure, and how to work with them to achieve your full potential by developing (BEQ). Expand and transform your business thinking and approach, by learning to recognize common, hidden emotional issues in a simple and straightforward manner. Strengthen your BEQ to achieve more accurate self-analysis, improved awareness, and effective functioning that creates predictable and positive results immediately.

Keywords

Emotional intelligence; career development; business success; career success; corporate politics; building career confidence; business agendas; business failure; business challenges; business strategies; business relationships; business mistakes; success strategies; business self improvement; workplace dysfunction; overcoming career obstacles; manipulative people; unhealthy corporate culture; business agendas; overcoming failure; difficult bosses; destructive coworkers; office politics; work failure and success; career coaching

Contents

Introduction

If you're not where you want to be in business, this book has the answer. It's a guide to building street-smarts and Business Emotional Intelligence (BEQ)—the ability, or operating system to recognize and manage effectively the challenging or destructive emotional tendencies, hidden agendas, and behaviors that emerge in the business environment.

Why is it critical that you apply yourself to building BEQ? Because, contrary to what we are routinely advised, business runs on emotion—yours and almost everyone else's. And that emotion is often negative, leading us into bewilderment, dysfunction, and failure.

We've all been told in countless ways that emotions—our feelings—have no place in the business process. And that's absolutely correct—at least to the extent that emotions are destructive to business and the people involved. But here is the dirty little secret, rarely if ever touched upon in business schools, and never fully acknowledged or discussed by professionals: *Business and its participants are held back, and sometimes totally crippled, by irrational and destructive feelings. Feelings that are often not only completely out of our conscious awareness, but at times completely out of our control.*

It's no wonder then that success and satisfaction are so elusive, when all of us have a hand, by ignoring emotional dynamics, in unknowingly dynamiting our progress, and the progress of the business we're in—every step of the way.

How did we get into this predicament? Simple—we were duped. By our teachers. By our mentors. By our parents. By the business community. Quite unintentionally, in most cases. They, along with society's rhetoric about business in general, have virtually brainwashed us into believing that business is an unemotional endeavor whose sole objective is to achieve profit and growth for the organizations and people involved. As a result, we typically assume emotional issues, particularly destructive ones, are not in play. A critical mistake. The truth is that emotions underlie and control virtually every aspect of business success or failure.

This book explains how and why emotions are a controlling factor in every career or business success and failure, and how you must work with them to achieve your full potential by building (BEQ). In fact, this book will expand and transform your business thinking and approach. It will guide you through common, hidden emotional issues in a simple and straightforward manner. You'll learn valuable concepts in developing BEQ, awareness, self-analysis, and effective functioning, so you can achieve predictable and positive results immediately. You will gain a competitive edge in business and will no longer be an unwitting victim of office politics, manipulation, or self-destructive behaviors—your own and other people's.

CHAPTER 1

Business and Your Emotional Agenda

What Is Emotional Intelligence in Business?

The concept of IQ or intelligence quotient is well understood. A set of standardized tests measure aspects of visual-spatial and auditory processing, as well as short-term memory and processing speed, to define a person's ability to solve problems across a range of tasks. We think of high-IQ individuals as smart problem solvers whose abilities we can measure.

But what about emotional intelligence or EQ? In the last couple of decades, thinkers and writers including, most famously, Daniel Goleman, the author of *Emotional Intelligence*, have explored why some people are gifted at managing the dynamics of interpersonal relationships and demonstrating emotional maturity, in their work and personal lives. Goleman and others identify traits that might define an individual as emotionally intelligent.

There is push-back, however, from the field of psychology. EQ, we are advised, is not a psychometrically valid concept. Insofar as it is anything, some psychologists suggest, it represents the Big Five trait agreeableness. Agreeable people are compassionate and polite, but they can also be pushovers. Disagreeable people, on average (if they aren't too disagreeable) make better managers, because they are straightforward, don't avoid conflict, and cannot be easily manipulated.

It's clear that clinical psychologists are staking out and protecting their turf, from what they consider to be pseudo-science, to uphold the integrity of psychometry, or the well-established science of measuring human traits and personality. But regardless of whether social scientists and psychologists approve of how EQ is conceptualized and measured as an aspect of human personality, it nevertheless continues to be a popular concept in mainstream culture that most people understand intuitively.

We all have friends, family, and colleagues who seem particularly gifted at managing relationships, resolving conflicts, oozing diplomacy, negotiating difficulties, inspiring confidence, promoting change, or who are simply superb at connecting and getting along with others to ensure successful outcomes.

The rest of us tend to speak of these types as being emotionally intelligent. Or street-smart, if they are particularly good at seeing through the games that people play in business, spotting the con artists, the tricksters, and the frauds. It's just a shorthand way of saying that some fortunate types combine a winning set of attitudes, traits, and behaviors that ensures them safer passage in the often stormy voyage of navigating relationships and circumstances at work and in life.

What about you? Do you consider yourself emotionally intelligent? Many of us do not. We struggle, which is why there are rafts of self-help and personal development books. We understand that managing emotions and getting along with others—what we unscientifically refer to as EQ—is essential for success, and we need to get better at it.

So what is Business Emotional Intelligence or BEQ? It's no more than understanding how identifying and managing emotional agendas in business, and seeing through deception, is every bit as important as having the knowledge and intellectual capacity to be a rational problem solver.

Why is BEQ especially important? Because many people commence their professional lives wrongfully assuming that rational thinking dominates the business landscape, and that emotion is banished or marginalized. Business, we are all taught, is led by managers, lawyers, and bean counters who run a tight ship, using clear objectives, rational and objective problem solving, and higher-order thinking. Wrong!

This could not be farther from the truth. Most of us have been privileged to work in healthy, constructive, and productive environments, where emotional acting out is at a minimum. Too often, however, we find ourselves in chaotic workplaces, run by dysfunctional bosses, who attract toxic employees. Culture, they say, eats strategy for breakfast, and sadly we consistently find ourselves stuck in business cultures that progress more along the lines of bad soap operas, than in functional organizations run by talented and emotionally mature professionals.

Unhealthy culture and dysfunction are why corporations often invest big dollars in organizational and leadership development, and personality testing, as business leaders and HR professionals try to avoid hiring the dysfunctional people who breed destructive environments.

It's a perennial problem, as witnessed by the sheer number of column inches and books that continue to mount, teaching us how to handle a difficult boss, avoid backstabbing colleagues, and navigate a dysfunctional workplace.

A Field Manual for Increasing Business Emotional Intelligence

In this book, BEQ is not presented as a scientific theory or formal approach to organizational development. It is simply a collection of useful strategies, insights, and directions, gleaned from veteran, street-smart business professionals, whose success has depended upon their ability to manage workplace dynamics and avoid the emotional mine fields that explode business progress.

This is a field guide of sorts on accepting that emotions are alive and well and wreaking havoc in business, and what to do about them. It's up to you to figure out how you tick emotionally. It's crucial that you learn how to manage yourself and others at work, so that your business interests are not undermined, and your professional goals are not sabotaged, by you, or some character with the power to torpedo your success. This book is here to help you.

We begin by looking inward. How many of us really understand how we actually work emotionally, and to what extent we irrationally process and react to what happens to us and around us? Most of us persist in self-destructive habits that confound us, repeatedly stubbing our toe and making the same avoidable mistakes over and over again.

We may take colleagues and friends at face value, believing we know them and can predict their actions, only to be blindsided and betrayed by behavior that we could not see coming. We enter into professional situations, investing in outcomes we feel sure of, only to watch them disintegrate before our eyes.

Business Emotional Intelligence and street-smarts evolve as we learn to be more discerning and perceptive in picking up on the emotional drivers in the business landscape. This gives us clues about who the players really are, under the surface, what agendas are at play, and how any situation is likely to evolve.

Business Emotional Intelligence often comes naturally with age and experience. Neuroscientists observe that after thousands of human interactions, a maturing brain becomes adept at a sort of pattern recognition. With just a few clues, interactions, or data points, we are, as we age, able to get what scientists call the "gist" of people or situations to predict outcomes more reliably.

But it's not practical to wait until we're long in the tooth to be able to assess circumstances correctly. Career success demands that we become as proficient at reading the tea leaves, so to speak, as accurately and as early on as possible. Some people never seem to learn, however. They may intelligently pile up information, but they continue to lack street-smarts or EQ. Their amassed knowledge or credentials don't necessarily make them any more capable of detecting destructive emotional undercurrents, which often sweep away the success that their analytical abilities predict is guaranteed.

Back to those personality tests. They are no doubt helpful in getting a handle on a professional's orientation, attitudes, and behaviors; strengths and weaknesses. But each of us is much more complicated than the results and analysis that emerge from any test we take. It's not so easy to pin us down. We're elusive. Each of us is a tricky and often unpredictable assortment of innate qualities, shaped by complicated life circumstances and personal history.

Jeff, a Harvard Law School graduate and seasoned lawyer, confessed a lifelong emotional struggle: "It's hard being a truth-telling people pleaser," he jokes half-heartedly. Jeff explained how he has a natural inclination to be forthright in presenting facts and well-timed insights, even if they are brutal. At the same time, growing up in a punishing household has left him irrationally afraid to deliver hard truths. His early experiences trained him to opt for telling people what they want to hear. This puts him in a troublesome bind: It is his job, and he is naturally predisposed, to speak

About the Author

WILLIAM KELLY

William Kelly is one of America's youngest voices in financial education, a portfolio entrepreneur, and fintech start-up founder dedicated to making investing more accessible to the next generation. He is also a co-host of the popular Boston radio programs *Safe Money Strategies* on WRKO 680 AM and *Saturday Night Safe Money Strategies* on WBZ 1030 AM, where he blends practical guidance with clear, relatable storytelling.

Born into a family business deeply rooted in financial planning, William grew up learning the principles of long-term wealth building from some of the industry's top professionals. By the time he was a teenager, he had already spent countless hours in client meetings, sharpening the skills and perspective that fuel his mission today: empowering young people to invest early and wisely.

A frequent traveler to Switzerland, England, Italy, Spain, and Canada, William draws inspiration from global markets and cultures. His experiences abroad, combined with nearly two years living in the Dominican Republic, shaped his passion for financial literacy as a tool for independence and opportunity.

Beyond finance, William is a powerlifter, youth coach, student, speaker, traveler, radio contributor, article contributor, philanthropist, advocate for libertarianism, and free market principles.

Only the Good Invest Young is his debut book, written to equip his peers with the confidence, strategies, and mindset to take control of their financial journeys.

truth forthrightly. At the same time, he harbors an irrational fear that doing so might upset others and result in him being "punished," as he was when growing up.

Confidence and Locus of Trust

Veteran football quarterback Joe Namath once proclaimed that "kick-ass confidence" is the key to success. But where does confidence, or faith in oneself, come from? A key component of confidence is being able to trust ourselves—our thinking, behavior, and decision making, even when we get it wrong and set ourselves up to learn a painful lesson. Locus of trust is just another way of saying "the place we put our trust." That place should be within ourselves whenever possible.

To be confident requires that we trust ourselves, but all too often in business, we are taught to put our trust elsewhere, in so-called experts. Our professional education, and preparation for life and career, often directs us to listen to others instead of to ourselves. High on the list of logical fallacies that undermine our thinking is what is known as "the appeal to authority fallacy"—taking what so-called experts say at face value, without using first principles to inquire for ourselves if a claim is actually true for us in our current situation.

Success arises from self-confidence, which emerges when we trust ourselves. This in turn develops when we learn how to challenge the ideas and beliefs of others, no matter how brilliant they might be, which have been handed down or passed to us, so that we can instead discover what is uniquely true for us. In the real world, not the world of theory, we must fall back on ourselves to make business and career decisions that dictate our future and whether or not we thrive or fail.

Let's Get Started: Learning to Deal With Hidden Realities That Get in Your Way

We are going to offer approaches to removing emotional blind spots that could be getting in your way, and to increasing your BEQ, in step-by-step fashion. First, we will explore the basic emotional challenges you will need to identify to overcome personal obstacles, some of which you may not be aware of. We will use real-world examples and case studies from the authors' personal experiences, as well as from interviews and encounters with other professionals. You will also be given exercises to hone your awareness and help knock down or end-run challenges that are impeding you, with the use of what we will refer to as a written development diary of sorts, written notes we suggest that you take from time to time. This will help you record and bring into clear focus any emotional blind spots, conscious or unconscious.

A Final Point

It's important when applying BEQ that you validate what does and does not work. Don't accept any idea or suggestion as true, until you have validated it through your own experience. This way you develop a strategy for success you can be sure works for you. Success comes from getting in touch with the part of you that *knows* how to succeed, and then finding techniques to validate this inner knowing. When results aren't favorable, you need to rethink what you're doing or what you've been told.

CHAPTER 2

The Emotional Challenge in Business

Confronting What We Believe

Gaining street smarts or upping our business game requires exploring and interrogating what we think we know, or blindly believe, to make sure wrong assumptions don't get in the way of our seeing clearly and acting appropriately. Let's talk about failure. We assume that failure is visited upon us against our will, and often it is. Some failures lie beyond our control.

At other times, however, failure is actually a choice, albeit an unconscious one. A choice cleverly hidden from view by a myriad of personal rationalizations. And obscured by received opinions and theories that we pick up from the business and management experts, and other influencers we're taught to heed. Keep the following in mind as you read: Success flows more naturally when you don't get in your own way. And the lack of success is often a choice—one that you don't have to make.

A Starting Premise

Emotions determine business results, so BEQ, is a must-have skill. Here's the reality: Virtually all business outcomes are dictated to a large extent by the emotional needs of those involved. A truth we rarely see or want to see until it's too late. This emotional blindness can undermine our business pursuits and decisions.

BEQ Case Study: An Incentive to Fail

Danny is a successful sales executive and consultant, who has made millions in the course of his career. A messy divorce sidelined Danny and forced him to divide his assets, giving his wife of many years half of his past and future earnings. After his divorce, and 30 years as a nonstop, hard-driving sales professional, Danny took a year off to tour the world, kick back, relax and play golf. But a nagging feeling told him that while he was still relatively comfortable financially, and having the time of his life in a more relaxed lifestyle, he should get back in the saddle and return to work.

Since age 12, Danny had worked multiple jobs to help support first his divorced mother and siblings, and later his wife and children. His work ethic and drive had pushed him into success as a relentless salesman, executive, and consultant. Working till it hurt was all that Danny had ever known, so even though he loved the new and more relaxed routine that he had earned with his blood sweat and tears, he berated himself and felt worthless. He was in his mid-fifties and energetic, but no longer productive. He was "goofing off," he told himself, and it had to stop.

Danny spun up a new sales management company. He hired Jonathan, a young, dynamic sales professional he had previously helped a client to recruit. Jonathan had impressed Danny so much that he made the younger man an offer to join his new company as a partner. "Working side-by-side, I know that we can consult to create world-class sales organizations to help turn around failing companies and earn good money," Danny told Jonathan, when he offered him the position. Jonathan had a wife, a mortgage and two small children, but he didn't think twice about jumping from his safe, well-paid, full-time sales position to join Danny. His new boss had an outstanding track record and reputation, and was willing to take him along for the ride.

The pair set up shop and new business inquiries soon poured in. They traveled the country and wrote proposals for a number of companies. Jonathan was excited but soon became perplexed. Danny was overpricing engagements, limiting the time they would commit, and making unrealistic demands of prospective clients. At a meeting that was supposed to clinch an assignment at a Cleveland software company, Danny told the hiring CEO that his input on his company's sales organization was neither welcome nor needed. Danny was the proven sales expert, and he wanted free reign. The deal, which had looked like a shoo-in, fell apart.

Initially, Jonathan had been happy to follow Danny's lead. After all, his partner was a master of sales ABCs—Always Be Closing—but after

THE EMOTIONAL CHALLENGE IN BUSINESS   9

six months, Danny's irrational behavior had lost the pair three major assignments. Danny was paying Jonathan a small monthly stipend, as they worked to land high-paying assignments, but it was not enough to cover his family expenses, or to replace the hefty salary he had sacrificed to jump aboard this new venture. Finally, after the dust-up with the CEO in Cleveland, Jonathan confronted Danny at the airport: "I feel like you are going out of your way to blow lucrative deals that we have both worked so hard to snag," he argued. Danny was furious and berated his junior partner for questioning him. Afterward, the pair sat in silence, waiting for their flights home.

The next day, after a sleepless night, still confused but apologetic, Jonathan called Danny to make amends. Danny stopped him: "Everything you said is correct," he said. "I am blowing deals." Danny, too, had stayed awake soul searching. He realized how much he resented returning to the familiar grind. Half of his future earnings would automatically go to his ex-wife, which made a grueling work schedule seem pretty fruitless from a financial standpoint.

More importantly, Danny realized how much he loved his new, more leisurely lifestyle, traveling and enjoying friends and new experiences. With some belt tightening, he knew he could afford his new routine, but work, he realized, had become a habit and unchallenged obligation. He had always felt that his role was to be a work horse, whether circumstances demanded it or not. The argument with Jonathan now forced Danny to admit that he no longer wished to work so hard, and this made him feel irrationally ashamed and like a failure.

Jonathan listened to Danny's explanation and had a solution: "You help bring in the work for a fee," he told Danny, "and let me hire someone to help execute the plans. You can oversee from the sidelines." It was a win-win. Danny was invaluable in attracting, winning, and steering new projects, while his younger partners had the willingness to work hard and implement them.

After a welcome break from his lifelong grueling schedule, Danny was unable at first to acknowledge that the role of workaholic was one that he now unconsciously resisted and rejected. He had failed to realize how much he hated the prospect of slipping back into such a demanding work schedule, which is why he had sabotaged new business opportunities.

Danny had set Jonathan and himself up to fail. The solution, going forward, was for him to reimagine success for himself, as an accomplished professional, who could still succeed, but by doing less, and relying more on others, to create the better work–life balance he had earned.

Emotional needs, good and bad, are in play across every aspect of the business process. When emotional agendas are destructive, failure is inevitable. When they're productive, success is likely. The people we encounter in business are handicapped at different rates by their lack of BEQ and how they apply it, and they challenge us accordingly in different ways.

CHAPTER 3

Destructive Agendas: The Hidden Business Killer

Waking Up to Emotional Reality

It can be taxing to remember throughout the business day that intelligently handling our own and other's emotions is a priority. We often instinctively look away from the relationship and emotional challenges we feel powerless to fix and instead focus on what we believe we can control.

Also stressful is coming to terms with an unfortunate reality: it's not always possible to do what is constructive and makes the best business sense. Destructive emotional agendas can block progress no matter what we do or say. And when this happens, realizing profits and pursuing the best course of action may become irrelevant and impossible. Not a welcome thought for anyone trying to do well.

In fact, certain business misconceptions, such as people are generally honest or want to do the right thing for the business, can be deeply embedded in our unconscious mind and prove downright misleading. Face up to this and understand that the thinking which held you back is not the thinking that will move you forward.

BEQ Case Study: Too Good to Be True

When Veronica first met Tony at a technology trade show in New York, she had an uneasy feeling. The fast-talking Long Islander sounded more like a hustler than a legitimate entrepreneur in the telecommunications industry. Her intuition was flashing red lights, but Tony won her over with tales of his accomplishments in business. He also asked her to join him for a series of phone conferences with high-profile businesspeople he claimed had been associates in his various business endeavors. Each of these impressive professionals seemed to know Tony, even if each one seemed in somewhat of a hurry to end their calls with him.

After three months, Veronica had taken Tony on as a client at her marketing firm. She agreed to forego a monthly retainer in return for a negotiated performance fee she would earn for helping Tony succeed in launching phone card services to underserved immigrant communities, a plan he called a no-brainer. Veronica introduced Tony to a lawyer friend, Rob. To fund their efforts, Rob helped unlock several bank accounts associated with Tony's prior business. Tony swore that he was only unable to access the accounts, because former, unethical partners had blocked him from his rightful earnings.

It all came crashing down one Tuesday morning, when Rob called Veronica to say they had both been duped by Tony, who had cleaned out the bank accounts they had helped him access. Tony had bolted with $80,000, which he was contractually prohibited from withdrawing, but had nevertheless taken. He was nowhere to be found.

Veronica called a couple of the people that Tony had introduced to her as close business allies. Both admitted that they considered Tony a scam artist and had ultimately brushed him off. But neither had wanted to expose him on the calls he had pestered them to take. Tony was a low-level con man, and Veronica and Rob, a Princeton Law School graduate, had fallen for the con. Veronica's gut had been right. She had sensed that Tony was not to be trusted. But three things had pulled her in, just as Tony, an accomplished manipulator, knew they would:

1. Tony promised Veronica and Rob a big pay-off from a surefire business deal, if they agreed to work for free and defer profit until later. Greed and the prospect of relatively easy money had overridden their better judgment.

2. Tony briefly introduced Veronica to credible business associates whom she failed to properly vet. This overrode her own negative impressions of Tony. People who are more successful than I seem to collaborate with him, so who am I to question his credibility, she had thought.

3. Tony had flattered Veronica, presenting himself as a street-smart operator, with lots of successful deals under his belt and savvy associates in his past. And he had chosen her to be a partner, albeit an unpaid one.

Fortunately, Veronica and Rob were not held accountable for the bank accounts that Tony had emptied, but Veronica nevertheless felt like she had dodged a bullet. The episode taught her not to second guess the inner voice that warned her when someone was bad news.

She had been brought up to believe that people were honest and to be trusted, so when Veronica's gut had screamed that Tony was shady, she had talked herself out of heeding the warning. It was an important lesson: If instinct tells you to be suspicious, listen and proceed carefully until trust and credibility are earned.

Accepting that counterproductive emotional needs or blind spots are everywhere in business and can block your ability to progress, signals that you're ready to spot when they may be getting in the way. And, once they have been identified, you'll learn to work around the ones you can't eliminate.

Examining Your Beliefs: The First Big Step

Moving forward may require continually examining every business-related belief you have. In doing this, however, expect that a part of you might resist seeing the landscape in a new way. You may want to block or reformat new insights to make them more palatable, but succumbing to this will keep you stuck.

As you read this book, expect to resist its content, openly mock, or grow annoyed, irritated, and even angry, at the ideas presented. You might think they sound simplistic, unrealistic, or unpalatable. "They don't apply to me," you will tell yourself. "I don't do these things." You may even want to put down the book and stop reading. Resist the urge.

Experiment with the notion that some material between these covers might be triggering an unconscious reaction to what you hear and shutting down your willingness to take on board uncomfortable truths that hide in plain sight. Take a chance and see any resistance or aversion as a clue that you should read on and contemplate what most of us, not surprisingly, want to shut out. Instead of swatting the ideas away, think long and hard about them, and actively investigate how your thinking and actions might indeed be hampered by the emotional blind spots we point out.

So, how do we break through?

- Begin by questioning every assumption and closely held belief that arises in a work or business setting.
- Create a clean slate of sorts to begin expanding your mental and emotional map and make way for fresh insight and successful new action.
- Accept that the people and circumstances before you may not be what you initially believe them to be.
- Consider the possibility that in a problem situation, you or an associate could unknowingly be undermining both your own efforts and theirs, even if this appears initially to make no sense. This opens you up to seeking solutions you might otherwise miss.

Spotting a Hidden Agenda

Later on, we'll explore the clues that tell us when hidden, destructive, or even unconscious emotions might be at play. Say, a manager hires an employee who is clearly unqualified for a job. On the face of it, this may make no business sense, but it does perhaps signify the manager's need to ward off threat or competition, or to control underlings. And it explains the common business expression that A players hire A+ players, while B players often hire C players.

Let's Take Your Emotional Temperature

Do you frequently consume news and gossip about high-profile or notable players in business or culture, and either marvel at or resent their success, maybe even gloating at their failures? A preoccupation with the illusion of how others are doing, which is decidedly different that the reality of their actual struggle, might indicate that you embrace escapism versus committing to the nuts and bolts process required to ensure your own success. It's easier to fantasize about the game than to engage with the realities of entering the arena and whole heartedly competing.

Not you? Ok, how about this? Do you often feel in awe when following the careers of wealthy or otherwise successful people and seek out the secrets of their success? Pro tips are useful, but they often fail to teach the step-by-step inner reasoning that ensures we process information in a dynamic situation and come to the proper conclusions that drive effective action. There is no one-size-fits-all solution to a problem. To prosper, you must find your own path and inner process, using your own innate gifts, and forget about relying on so-called business gurus to spoon feed you answers.

One more question: Do you ever find yourself holding beliefs that you never challenge? Beliefs that come from other people and not from your own experience, such as the classic, it's hard to succeed in business? Or to succeed you must have a special education or go to a top college? Or be in the right place at the right time? Or have a powerful network? Of course, all of these can be valuable assets, but the truth is that there is a unique path you can walk, which, with the proper mindset, will lead to your success. And beyond intelligence and hard work, applying BEQ to your work life is key to carrying the day.

BEQ Awareness Tip: The key to expanding our mental and emotional map for business success begins by questioning ingrained beliefs and assumptions. And beginning to look inward to understand, in exquisite detail, how we process and transact in our business life.

Never Forget: If You Have the Desire You Almost Certainly Have the Talent

There's absolutely no doubt that if you have a strong desire to achieve a particular business or career goal, you probably have the talent and ability to achieve it. We are often passionate about the things we love to do, work hard and excel at, so it's time to clear the true obstacles from your path, including low BEQ, that leads you to ignore or mismanage tough emotional realities.

While it's not possible to generalize about what the particular road-blocks to your progress may be, it's likely that a major contributing factor is a failure to venture outside of your emotional comfort zone. This may show up, for example, as a tendency to be intimidated and avoid working with dynamic hard-chargers who make things happen in business, because this might shine a light on bad feelings or personal inadequacies you harbor about yourself. If this is the case, push forward, and where possible, run with energetic, success-oriented go-getters. You'll soon discover that many of the uncomfortable feelings that make you want to hide out instead of engaging will fall away.

BEQ Case Study: Professional Security Blanket

Elaine was a young and rising star in public relations, who left the top boutique Manhattan firm, where she had been a standout, to strike out on her own. Tom, a former client, heard about Elaine's move to start her own firm and invited her to pitch him and his partners, who had set up a new auditing business.

Elaine had excelled at winning lucrative, high-profile accounts, but that was when she had an entire agency staff backing her. Alone, as she was now a solo practitioner, Tom and his team were grilling her in the conference room. Elaine lost her nerve. She flopped. The meeting ended and Tom walked her to the elevator. "What happened?" he asked her. "I was sure you could win this crowd over in your sleep." Elaine blurted out the truth: "I'm afraid," she said. "I don't think I can do it all by myself. And you were all looking at me as though everything I suggested was completely off base."

"Your ideas were great," Tom reassured her,

> but you seemed so unsure of yourself. Don't be afraid. Your talent hasn't disappeared just because you're no longer part of a large team. Write up a proposal and include all the creativity you are famous for, and I know I can bring the others around.

Elaine won the business and took up the new account. She had lost the security blanket of a supporting organization, but even though she was now working solo, she realized that her talent was not diminished. And the thrill of being her own boss and following her own instincts in managing an account for success was more rewarding than life as an employee in a larger operation.

A BEQ *Awareness Exercise*

Over the next week, be open to the *possibilities* that:

- People in business often act in self-destructive ways.
- Business decisions are emotionally driven and can put profit, growth, or career progress at risk.

Jot down these two possibilities and review them at the start of each business day in your Development Diary. As you go through the day, make a note of any resistance to these ideas, as you consider they might be true in actual work situations. This will put you in touch with cognitive dissonance—or the conflict that occurs when reality contradicts our beliefs about the way things are.

CHAPTER 4

The Basics About Emotions in Business

The Powerful Role Emotions Play in Business

We're all driven in our personal lives, sometimes unknowingly, uncontrollably and irrationally, by our emotional needs. The same is true in our business lives. If you're in business and cannot see the powerful grip that emotions, particularly destructive or nonproductive ones, have on everyone around you, including yourself, then lost income, lost opportunity, and lack of progress are guaranteed.

Unhealthy emotional needs drive a whole range of counterproductive behaviors from people who might:

- Impulsively quit jobs;
- Kill business deals;
- Chronically miss deadlines;
- Show up late for work;
- Fail to return phone calls;
- Become argumentative;
- Refuse overtime;
- Renege on promises;
- Dominate meetings;
- Criticize others; and
- Talk too much.

And the list goes on.

BEQ Case Study: An Inability to Listen

Jeremy was an expert business strategist. More than that, he was typically the hardest-working person on any team he joined. He unfailingly crunched data and thought long and hard about how to design effective solutions. But Jeremy had a fatal flaw that almost killed his career: he was incapable of really listening to others. In almost every meeting, Jeremy interrupted and stepped on others when they spoke, seemingly oblivious to their contributions.

Colleagues could see in his eyes that Jeremy was barely listening to them, no matter how qualified or senior they might be. He was simply waiting for his chance to speak again, and the sooner the better. Some saw his behavior as arrogance. Others saw it as anxiety. Jeremy seemed so eager to share the valuable content he had worked hard to develop that he literally couldn't take in what others were saying. The outcome of this bad habit was always the same: Although Jeremy was smart, others felt disrespected by him, and few managed to develop a productive rapport with him, aside from leveraging his necessary input for a given project.

Throughout his career, numerous bosses gave Jeremy important feedback on changing his bad habit. And later, after he went into business for himself, clients and associates delivered the same message. "For heaven's sake, can you stop interrupting and let someone else speak?" one client scolded Jeremy during a tense conference call. Jeremy was momentarily silent, but soon returned to his familiar ways.

An overriding impulse to talk and not adequately listen hurt Jeremy in business, costing him relationships and revenue. But Jeremy was either unwilling or unable to change. Dominating every conversation and meeting, as though he were the smartest and most worthy person involved, remained Jeremy's primary driver and need, no matter the cost to his professional well-being or bank account.

Ringing any bells? Starting to recognize the stranglehold that counterproductive motivations might have?

A Ground Floor Insight

The need for big a pay-day, power, attention, the spotlight, recognition, and control, all acted out in the business arena, are driven by emotional needs. Think about it. And if you find yourself continually losing to other people's office politics, or emotionally manipulative business tactics, you're not applying BEQ correctly. Unfortunately, in business, the statement "Nice guys finish last" is often true, in a sense. It really should be "Unaware guys finish last."

BEQ Awareness Challenge: Often business or staff meetings run according to a published agenda, and most of us tend to assume that all participants are there to follow this agenda. The next time you attend a meeting, stop and ask yourself if you have any underlying or hidden motivations: perhaps to be noticed by a supervisor? To get even with a colleague who undermined you? To make sure you get rightful credit for an idea that is working well, but few are aware you initiated.

How about other attendees? Go around the room and silently try to guess what each person is preoccupied with, or might be trying to accomplish in terms of a personal agenda. It matters little whether your guesses are right or wrong. What counts is that you challenge your assumptions and prescribed thinking to understand that business objectives always sit side by side with the emotional needs of the people involved in achieving them.

Managing Your Process

Reaching your business goals, whether negotiating a deal, setting up a branding strategy, building a business, or getting promoted, requires recognizing the emotional undercurrents at play within the people and situations you encounter. And you must assess and manage your own emotional process, making sure you unblock yourself by removing the filters, received opinions, attitudes, and incorrect beliefs about business that have been passed on to you and which often contradict real-world experience. Learning to view yourself and others more honestly, despite built-in resistance, demonstrates high BEQ.

There is no surefire way to change the emotionally driven actions of people who may be thwarting you. Confronting their bad behavior will not be met with open arms or even acknowledged. The hard truth is that you can change only how you think and how you act. Think of business as a card game. If you suspect someone is cheating, you have only two choices: get out of the game, or play absolutely no-holds-barred, within the limits of your personal integrity, to win.

BEQ Case Study: Fear of Being Honest

Robert was head of finance at a struggling mid-sized distributor of medical equipment. After the turnover of two CEOs in just two years, the company's board hired yet another CEO, on a three-month trial, to make sure the fit was right. "I trust your feedback," the board sponsor told Robert. "If you think this guy is a bad match, I want you to tell me before we convert him to the permanent CEO role."

John, the new CEO, was talented, but displayed a thinly veiled ego that was more about command and control than respecting and nurturing the management team he had joined. This egotism and several other traits did not sit well with Robert, but he felt guilty for holding such a negative opinion of the new CEO. It's a tough job, Robert thought. I should cut the guy some slack as he tries to get the company back on the right track.

Even though he felt uneasy, Robert gave the thumbs up on John's permanent appointment to CEO, when the board asked him for his final verdict and feedback. No sooner was the ink dry on John's permanent contract than he threw off the façade of agreeableness and revealed himself to be the self-dealing tyrant his previous behavior had suggested. Within six months, Robert and several other key managers had their resumes out, seeking new positions.

Robert mentally reviewed the last few months. If he were honest with himself, he could see that he had correctly read the writing on the wall in strongly suspecting that John was not an effective leader. But he had been unwilling or unable to trust his instincts and be brutally honest in his feedback to the board. Robert had wanted to be "fair" to John, who in turn showed himself to be ruthless and self-serving.

The Challenge of Hidden Emotions

Identifying and acknowledging hidden emotional motivations or unhelpful tendencies is hard and sometimes painful. In the beginning, it takes a persistent effort.

BEQ Awareness Challenge: We are seldom awake or brave enough to confront the true motivations and games being played by those around us. Neither are we fully aware of our own unconscious needs, which often includes acting out what we, like Robert in the previous example, mistakenly think we should be doing in business, versus what is actually in the best interests of ourselves and others.

Most of us want to avoid disappointment at all costs, and yet we may find ourselves expecting or bracing for it. Unconsciously anticipating disappointment or failure distracts us from focusing single mindedly on achieving success. A tendency to hedge can undermine our efforts and rob us of victory.

A solution: Where possible, adopt the absolute conviction that you will succeed. If you can't do this, at least try to remain relaxed, curious and open minded, rather than fearful and negative, about potential outcomes. Embrace fearlessness as a way to stay open to new paths and possibilities, even the ones that intimidate you. As Eleanor Roosevelt famously advised, "Do one thing every day that scares you."

One successful real estate entrepreneur shared his approach to acting boldly and decisively:

> Every day, I build my fear muscle. I take well calculated risks that often feel too big and daring and outside my comfort zone. Nevertheless, I strive to remain convinced that any new deal will work out. If I can't sustain optimism, I at least try to adopt an attitude of curiosity instead of fear or dread. Being curious, instead of worrying, is how I keep at bay the anxiety that would otherwise stop me from taking action and making progress. If a project fails, at least I get to learn an important lesson about what does or does not work.

Why We Turn a Blind Eye to Destructive Emotional Issues

Facing the truth about hidden agendas is not only uncomfortable, but it can also even be frightening, particularly when our financial security is at stake. All of us know it's virtually impossible to deal with an irrational person, so is it any wonder that we want to look away from those who are irrational, when our livelihood or well-being is in some way dependent on what they do and how they act. And what about when we are being irrational and getting in our own way?

The party line that emotions have no place in business is self-serving denial. Who, after all, wants to admit that hard work, common sense, talent, and logic may not be enough to guarantee success? But it's undeniable that those driven by emotion and ego needs over reason often control a deal, a department, or even the whole show. Take Mr. Doomsday for example.

Doomsday Thinkers

Have you ever worked with someone who continually criticizes everyone and everything? Or been in a meeting where someone, let's call him Mr. Doomsday, finds endless reasons why a solid new business idea won't work? If so, did you notice how these negative types often succeed in killing a viable idea or bringing the business discussion to an absolute and frustrating halt? More importantly, did you wonder why such people are allowed to push their negative views and get away with it, because others typically don't push back? The answer is that negative players often infect groupthink.

It's difficult to remain optimistic and open minded in the face of relentless skepticism and negativity. Teams sense that when there is not universal commitment to making an idea work, it will fail. Another version of this is when those team players, who do not support an idea, only pay lip service to implementing it in meetings, while actively undermining the strategy in their ongoing efforts.

Several years ago, the *Harvard Business Review* cited this behavior of playing along, without sincere effort and commitment, as a key indicator of business failure: Teams might appear to reach consensus and commit to implementing a business strategy, only to have it fail, because skeptical, resentful, or negative team members don't back up their reluctant agreement with the effort required for success. In fact, they often work secretly to sabotage teamwork and undermine those who champion the project.

So what motivates the doomsday types? Sometimes they may genuinely disagree with the consensus opinion or the validity of a business idea. In other instances, a Mr. Doomsday is anxiety ridden, cripplingly risk-averse, and afraid of failure. It's easier to shoot down a viable idea than to live with the persistent worry that it might fail. The doomsday types may look good on paper, with the right education and resume, but in reality, they hobble their own career prospects and stymie the hard chargers around them.

Another reason we may be reluctant to call out another's negative behavior is that they are doing our dirty work for us. Maybe we too are afraid of failure, and so it is easy to hide behind the person who speaks up and voices the doubts and fear we secretly harbor. Now we have a partner in the crime of not trying or risking. We don't have to question our own fear of failure. We can take refuge in other doomsday complainers, who are sure that a good idea won't work. Congratulations! That's one more business risk or opportunity to succeed that you don't have to take up!

CHAPTER 5

Society's Indoctrination and Mistaken Beliefs

When the Well-Intentioned Mislead Us

Before we have the requisite knowledge or experience to guide our work endeavors, we turn to parents, teachers, or associates we think can help us. Unfortunately, we often don't stop to consider if they have the proper qualifications. Put another way—have they actually succeeded at the task or challenge we face?

Too often, they are handing down shop-worn wisdom, best guesses, theory that has never been tested or has resulted in failure. Without thinking, we uncritically take on board bad advice from people we mistakenly trust, and use it as part of the operating manual for our professional life. We fail to ask the hard question, "Why should I listen to you?"

Hans Christian Andersen children's story about the Emperor's New Clothes is a good metaphor for our reluctance to question, think for ourselves, and forthrightly venture an honest opinion: The emperor was told by two cheats, masquerading as weavers, that they could make him uncommonly beautiful clothes, which would be invisible to those who were too stupid for office and visible only to the wise. The delighted emperor commissioned new clothes from the cheats. In time, they presented him with invisible garments, knowing that the emperor and his advisors would be too afraid of appearing stupid to voice the truth that the clothes did not exist. When a naked emperor set out in a procession through the town, only a child, unafraid to tell the truth, called out what everyone was thinking, but dare not say—that the emperor was naked.

So many business professionals are afraid to speak up and announce that the emperor has no clothes—that a person, idea, or critique has no substance and is going in the wrong direction. It's often too easy to just follow the herd in a misguided effort, bad call, or avoidable failure.

Three of the most feared and least used words in business are "I don't understand." Ironically, the more accomplished and sure of their instincts that professionals become, the more they are able to announce honest reservations politely but firmly. They are comfortable in forthrightly proclaiming that they do not understand specific support or criticism for a particular idea or business direction. Practice being true to your inner voice that questions, even if you don't have the answers. And as you do, get used to colleagues pulling you to one side to say, "I am glad you spoke up. You said exactly what I was thinking."

BEQ Awareness Tip: When you find yourself struggling in business, review all of the entrenched beliefs and attitudes you may be basing your decisions upon, especially beliefs from others that you swallowed without proper questioning. Be prepared to sweep such received opinions aside and seek guidance from more reliable sources. Or listen more closely to your own instincts and common sense.

A Particular Risk for Would-Be Entrepreneurs

Irrational or misguided beliefs create a particular risk for people who dream of owning their own business. Would-be entrepreneurs often rationalize why they can't start or succeed in their own venture, undercutting their efforts by not giving it their all. Or by giving up before they even get started. It can be psychologically more comfortable to talk oneself out of a new business than to go all in, try hard, and still have it fail. Getting started as an entrepreneur requires new emotional habits:

- *Stay flexible.* Successful entrepreneurs and professionals are able to keep a handle on the anxieties and fears that crowd their mind. They remain flexible and able to take detours around unexpected challenges, since most businesses or careers, especially new ventures, seldom conform to preset plans and expectations.
- *Stay focused on the goal and expect twists and turns on the path.* Those who fail often have an irrational need for results to unfold according to their grand plan and set timetable—their

imagined benchmark for success. It's not where you start, it's where you finish, and those who steadfastly pursue their initial aims in the face of problems, understanding that there will always be detours, unexpected challenges, and lucky breaks, reach their goals. Looking back, they see that by hanging in, even when the going got tough, they were always on track for success.

- *Be open to failure.* Have you heard the claim that if you don't fail big by the age of 40, you may never really succeed? If you're a would-be entrepreneur who finds yourself endlessly mulling over fear of failure, this can be clue that you are looking for ways to fail before you even start, because real-world failure is intolerable to you. Failure may feel unacceptable, but it is necessary in building resilience, learning lessons, and adopting a realistic view of how life and business actually work.

- *Analyze data and gather useful insights.* This is a worthwhile exercise to inform yourself and help gauge your chances for success, when you enter the business arena as an entrepreneur or hard-charging professional. If your underlying emotional makeup is such that you cannot tolerate failure, however, you may misuse data and research as a way to foster face-saving rationales and talk yourself out of really trying. Sticking with the status quo ensures you don't court failure, but it also limits your chances of finding success.

BEQ Case Study: Finding the First Step

Nico had worked for the family construction business as a project manager since he left high school. By the age of 25, he was craving new challenges and the chance to escape working for his father, who was kind and fair, but tended to manage Nico, as though he were a know-nothing kid, rather than an experienced professional.

For two years, Nico contemplated new directions and took various courses: web design, computer programming, real estate sales, even bookkeeping. Every month he had drinks with his best friend, Simon, and shared all the bold ideas he had to get out of working for the family and onto a new career path. Finally, Simon had heard enough. "Nico, you are full of good intentions, but you are not willing to follow through on even one of them. You are chopping and changing, committing to nothing."

Nico was initially stunned by his friend's honesty. He mulled over his dilemma for weeks, until he finally uncovered the issue plaguing him: he had no confidence. Rationally, he knew that he was effective in his job, but the truth was that few people outside his family had witnessed his ability to perform. Instead of being too ambitious in pursuing radical new career directions, Nico realized that the critical first step he needed to take was to build his confidence, by making career changes that were realistic and manageable.

Within a few weeks, Nico had plucked up courage to take a job, as an account manager with a plumbing supply company, where he had routinely bought supplies in his previous role. It was the first step in standing on his own two feet outside the family business, and Nico knew he could build fresh skills and a new vision of himself in the new position.

Understanding the precise next step we must take to get ourselves unstuck requires emotional honesty in confronting the fears, concerns, or blocks that often lie below the surface of awareness. We are not always emotionally ready for the ambitious directions we determine to take. Taking both practical and emotional considerations into account frees us up to make the appropriate move comfortably.

The Emotional Challenge Can Be Different for Men and Women

As a rule, though not always, men are socialized to suppress their feelings more than women. Consequently, men are often uncomfortable dealing with displays of emotions, or when they believe feelings are at play in a business setting. So much so that some men will aggressively criticize anything that they perceive as less than rational, factual, and levelheaded. A problem with this approach is that their so-called rational thinking can sometimes be little more than their own clever rationalization of hidden emotional needs or irrational and counterproductive wants. Emotion masquerading as logic.

Accessing and expressing feelings generally comes more easily for women. Gut feelings about a business idea or potential business partner can be extremely valuable. But this can create a dilemma, particularly around those men (and women), who might be convinced that feelings or intuition don't belong in the business process. So, the challenge for women and men who rely more on intuition, feelings, or tacit data, is not to feel intimidated into shutting down their hunches. But instead to find a rationale or comfortable way of expressing instinct so that it is palatable to colleagues.

Distorting Reality: A Major Risk

When our personal psychology or lack of BEQ distorts or blocks us from witnessing what's actually happening in business, we become factually blind. In effect, we develop emotional *blind spots* that stop us from noticing and dealing with dynamics, relationships, and actions that are steering us off course. We put a lid on our innate abilities. Our full business potential is never reached.

On the other hand, if your psychological makeup has you comfortable with success, open to attaining it, and even sure that you will, then success is built into your emotional groundwork. And the chances are that you do not harbor a hidden saboteur, who is there to take you out or collaborate with others in hobbling you.

So, what does this all mean for your BEQ? Simply, do not suppress, or run away from, unwanted thoughts or feelings, no matter how uncomfortable, even when they don't make sense to you. If you do, you miss the extent to which your own or someone else's emotional issues may be supporting or interfering with your career.

CHAPTER 6

Handling Difficult People

Successful People Sense Right Action

No one, not even the most successful among us, escapes interference or meddling from others, but street-smart professionals with higher BEQ have improved strategies for dealing with troublemakers.

If you suspect a colleague or associate, even one you are friendly with, might be jeopardizing your progress, trust the feeling, but don't react immediately. Take your time and be alert to concrete indications and clues that support your gut instinct. We'll talk more about clues later. For now, above all, don't take anything that is said or done personally. If you do, and you react defensively or angrily, *you'll compromise your ability to handle the situation effectively.*

BEQ Case Study: Managing a Sixth Sense

Paula was a very intuitive operations manager. Sometimes it was as if she could read the mind of the person sitting across from her. And why not? Experts confirm that 97 percent of all communication is nonverbal. Paula wasn't 100 percent correct in her hunches, but correct enough to assess who was a sincere friend or ally, and who was a competitor putting on a false front. Paula could intuit what people were up to, and pick up on innuendo, insinuations, or clues that someone was undermining her or playing politics.

Paula's problem was that she tended to blurt out too soon likely truths that others were still oblivious to. Like a modern-day Cassandra, a prophetess in Greek mythology who was destined never to be believed, Paula often pointed out what others could not yet see. She was expert at reading subtext—information that lies below the surface—and immediately confronting others with it.

But colleagues were often unable to see what Paula had already accurately sensed. As a result, she had to fight the reputation that she was too speculative and political. Nevertheless, those who knew her well grew to trust her instincts and read on business situations, personalities, and dynamics.

Finally sensing that she was doing herself no favors with her soothsaying and truth telling, Paula worked with a coach. She learned to keep track of her impressions, until she had a complete picture of what was taking place. And only when associates began raising questions and looking for answers or clarity about a given situation, did Paula step forward, confident that others were now willing to see what she had already known for some time. A good leader is someone who can assess a situation and think ahead, but who also knows how to wait for others to catch up. Paula eventually mastered this leadership skill, and used her "golden gut" as an asset not a liability.

Side Stepping Traps

In handling the difficult people we inevitably encounter in all areas of business, from bosses to colleagues, associates, clients and negotiating partners, consider the following:

- *Don't Fall into the Trap.* Never forget, emotionally challenging or destructive players are experts in fostering an agenda. Invariably, their strategy, conscious or unconscious, is to bait you into being openly reactive, so they can then point to you as being emotional or unprofessional. Such people often deal in subtext: innuendo, unspoken hostility, or roadblocking that is so subtly directed as not to be picked up by others. Your calling attention to what others cannot see, or haven't noticed, runs the risk of making you appear divisive, negative, or like a poor team player. Flushing out the game, as Paula did, to make what is hidden visible to others takes skill.
- *Calmly Point Out Facts.* Always simply state facts about what is actually occurring in any veiled conflict. Don't waste your time accusing a colleague you suspect of manipulating

a situation to your disadvantage. If a competitive boss stonewalls you or is stingy with support, it does no good to point out that they seem invested in seeing you fail. Instead, state the truth, as matter of factly as possible. For example, "I don't seem to be getting feedback or any confirmation from you about the pros and cons of the project I am working on. Am I misreading this?"

Adopting the Proper Mindset

Cultivate BEQ by taking on board the following suggestions:

- *Acknowledge You Are in Control.* Your business destiny is fully under your control, and you have the power to overcome challenges, seek out constructive partners, and sidestep saboteurs, or those who are simply unhelpful.
- *Acknowledge the Possibility of Personal Blind Spots.* Most of us are aware, in some measure, of the many topics we know little or nothing about. But very few are willing to contemplate how much there is that "we do not know that we do not know," especially as it pertains to our personal makeup. Be 100 percent committed to uncovering personal blind spots on a daily basis, even when it means facing up to what temporarily alarms or discourages you. What you don't know about yourself, and remains hidden, can sink you. What am I missing? What can't I see? should always be uppermost in your thinking.
- *Know You Can Eliminate Your Roadblocks.* Never doubt for a moment that, with persistence, you can grow out of low BEQ, and the conscious or unconscious hang-ups that are holding you back.
- *Don't Blame Yourself for Your Roadblocks.* BEQ is a skill that we commit to building once we accept that we need it. Some people possess naturally high BEQ. We've all met the type. They effortlessly perform in the game at hand, managing people, conflict, intrigue, disappointment, and setbacks with

incredible ease. The rest of us are often saddled with unhelpful secondhand information, instincts that we've been taught to downplay, intelligence that goes untapped, and a faulty belief system. It never occurs to us to take people and situations at anything other than face value. Analyzing what is really going on to understand hidden dynamics, agendas, gameplaying, and power struggles takes practice.

- *Don't Try to Change Anyone Else.* Never believe that you can change anyone else. It's a waste of time and shows a failure to grasp reality. You can only change yourself. So, if you're struggling, there is only one person that you need to tackle— *you.* And that means changing the misguided beliefs that you have about yourself and how you have to perform to achieve your goals.
- *Believe You Have the Talent.* Don't fall into the trap of believing that you are not where you want to be because you lack ability. If you are hard working with reasonable intelligence, all that is missing is Business EQ, and your willingness to increase it.

With these suggestions in mind, you can set the table for improved performance. Operating with BEQ takes practice and can be stressful. It's a different, savvier, and street-smart way of entering the business landscape and engaging.

Moving Forward—Your Awareness Journey

As we've suggested, when our emotional makeup allows us to accept success, we immediately, and sometimes unconsciously, move in a direction that increases our chances of success. On the other hand, when our emotional makeup does not allow us to accept success, we fail.

Next let's begin the process of enhancing your sensitivity to underlying emotional dynamics in business. To do this, it's not necessary to understand the psychological factors that may undergird emotional issues. In fact, at times, trying to figure out why, for example, we work for an offensive boss, or why someone runs a particular company poorly, may actually prevent us from dealing fully with the reality of what we have encountered and taking corrective actions. It's the old story: If you focus too intently on the details, you will lose sight of the big picture.

As you grow more aware of your own hidden feelings, you will be more alert to how those you deal with may experience similar feelings or insights. This can be of immeasurable help in relating well and winning the cooperation of others who can aid you.

CHAPTER 7

Getting Comfortable With Being Uncomfortable

The Comfort Zone Challenge

Whether we realize it or not, we all tend to manipulate or reformat what we see, in order to stay in our comfort zone, and avoid facing uncomfortable realities that contradict our world view. We're always confronting problems in business and life that, in reality, should be pretty simple to solve, but which, nevertheless, go unsolved. An old colleague used to call these "unsolvable solvable problems." Why do they go unsolved? Usually it's because what masquerades as a problem is actually satisfying some individual or group agenda that overrides stated business goals.

Take Nancy, a credit executive. She is talented, but known for a massive flaw: She hires friends and associates who, she believes, support and like her, whether they are right for a particular position or not. FON—Friends of Nancy—is how colleagues describe the retinue that follows Nancy from job to job. Nancy needs familiar faces around her. Time might be wasted, and performance, while good, might be suboptimal, because staying comfortable and unthreatened is more important to Nancy than finding the best, not the most familiar, candidate for the job.

We see the same resistance to pursuing effective solutions throughout society and politics at large. Politicians might use immigration or economic or health care policy as wedge issues to fight and beat their opponents in elections. Everyone understands that the Congress and the Senate could come together in compromise to negotiate helpful if imperfect solutions to serious challenges facing the country. But the fact is that creating fear and outrage about an opponent's positions satisfies the politician's pressing personal agenda of getting elected and securing personal or partisan power.

Sticking With Our Script

We each have a vision of the world, ourselves, our professional life, and our place in it. Based on internal scripting, this view of who we can be, and what we can achieve, is often limited and not ambitious enough. It is the rare person who dreams a big dream and pursues it whole heartedly. A career coach captured this when she observed that most people are not trained to move toward what they want but to back away from what they do not want. We too often lack confidence or daring, and are fearful about confronting an uncomfortable challenge and breaking through. It's easier to go in reverse and avoid the conflict.

Successful people with high BEQ learn how to suspend limiting self-judgments, expectations, ego needs, and fear of rejection or failure. They move in as straight a line as possible toward their goals, breaking through the barriers, not taking no for an answer, not worrying about maintaining a particular self-image, and not avoiding necessary upset.

How about you? Is your controlling desire to maintain your carefully constructed story of who you think you are and how you think the world works? If so, then anything that contradicts this is a threat. We choose not to solve those solvable unsolvable problems because the price it too great. We don't want to relinquish safe assumptions and illusions about ourselves, so we forego living up to our potential. Waking up to the fact that we ourselves are the primary cause of our disappointment and failures give us the best chance of correcting our situation.

The Consequences of Choosing Comfort Over Reality

OK, so we're led astray when our primary focus is on staying emotionally comfortable and not confronting mistaken beliefs about ourselves and others. Let's say you found out that a coworker cheats on her expenses while on business trips. How you feel about this behavior can clue you in to personal needs or illusions. None of us wants to stand in moral judgment, and we accept that no one is perfect, but your explaining away a colleague's dishonesty means you may not face up to her bad behavior in other areas, including her dealings with you.

If a colleague is willing to cheat the company, will they cheat you? Probably. Because cheating shows a willingness to rationalize bad behavior to bolster personal interests. So, if you were to get between an associate and some benefit they felt they deserved or wanted, perhaps they would sell you out, too, writing off their dubious actions as necessary.

If you do catch others lying, cheating, or manipulating and find yourself making excuses, or telling yourself that you want to focus on the good in others instead of finding fault, you're hampering your ability to take care of yourself.

Some professionals inadvertently block their progress by chronically judging themselves unfairly. Nothing they do or have is ever good enough. What never occurs to them is that continually belittling themselves and their performance is merely one way to languish in a state that is unpleasant but familiar, at the expense of trying for more happiness and success. It's low BEQ that maintains a distorted view of the world, in which our primary agenda is counting all the ways that we don't measure up.

A BEQ Awareness Development Task

The next time you talk to someone who obviously performs well in some area, perhaps they are a hard worker or a good parent or accomplished musician, compliment them and pay attention to the response. Do they accept the compliment graciously or instead downplay or even reject it? What do you glean from their answer? Do you see yourself reflected in their behavior? Notice how we continue to give each other clues about ourselves, our self-image, and emotional outlook.

Quick Analysis

People who are overly focused on their flaws, and constantly seeking evidence of their poor performance, continually put themselves down. Compliments challenge their low opinion of themselves and move them out of their safe space. This might be grounded in not wanting to outperform a father, mentor, or idealized figure. Or in a belief that they can never grow beyond humble or limited beginnings—an impostor syndrome of sorts. "I just can't get there from here," an internal critic tells them.

If you think you have a warped or unrealistic view of yourself, consider building a credible trust circle of people you feel comfortable asking to critique your strengths and weaknesses, or handling of a particular situation. As part of building your BEQ, learn to replace inaccurate self-perceptions with more objective feedback from others. Maintaining a realistic view of our strengths and weaknesses means we don't waste time on chronic misperceptions or misapprehensions, so we can advance more efficiently.

Emotional Blind Spots

We listen to news every day that describes event after event in which people lie, cheat, steal, and abuse others for personal gain. Who are these culprits? Are they from another planet? Are we to believe that, of all the people we encounter in business, none falls into this category? This false assumption puts us at risk.

Furthermore, we tend to believe that we have thoroughly evaluated an associate long before we have seen enough to accurately predict how they might behave or perform.

Thinking we know someone well, when we don't, keeps doubts and suspicions under wraps where we don't have to wrestle with them. A rush to judgment, and giving others unearned trust too quickly, exposes us to risk that can cost us money, opportunity, and peace of mind. Sometimes it can even take years before circumstances reveal an associate's true character.

BEQ Case Study: A Hidden Bully

The heavy stapler came sailing past Lisa's ear, barely missing her. It had been hurled by her business partner, Joanne. Before setting up an advertising agency together two years earlier, Lisa and Joanne had worked informally together for over 10 years on creative projects, as a copywriter and graphic designer respectively. Pulling each other into the various jobs that one or the other found, they collaborated so successfully that eventually they decided to set up an official partnership.

Lisa had two young children and was taking care of a sick parent. She wanted to start out their new venture by working from her small home office to keep expenses low until the two partners were sure that their business would take off. Joanne was more grandiose. She wanted to rent loft space and fill it with expensive equipment and a growing staff. In fact, Joanne quickly found and rented a spacious loft, over Lisa's objections, close to her own home, but at some distance from Lisa's.

"I'll come in and work in the new space whenever I can," Lisa explained. "But I have too much on my plate, and I can get just as much work done at home. Plus, I think we should build the business slowly and avoid crippling ourselves with needless stress and obligations." Joanne pressured Lisa to cosign the three-year lease for the office splurge, but Lisa managed to stand her ground and not sign. Joanne was unhappy about this, and with each passing month, she became more and more critical of Lisa, flying into rages over the smallest disagreement or perceived infraction.

Lisa was baffled. During the ten years that they had collaborated informally, she had never seen this side of Joanne, who had always seemed so good natured and thoughtful. More and more, Lisa found herself giving in to Joanne's temper tantrums, neglecting responsibilities at home, and wasting time on commuting to the office, simply because Joanne demanded it.

On the morning that the stapler almost hit her, Lisa had been up most of the night, tending to her sick mother. She had called in to apologize for missing an early morning meeting and rushed into the office as soon as her sister had arrived to spell her at home, only to be met with Joanne's fury. Exhausted, shaken after barely escaping a head injury, and sick of Joanne's bullying, Lisa blew up and gave Joanne the tongue lashing that she had been holding back for months. She then turned and walked out. It was the last straw. The partnership was over.

Later that day, Joanne called, explaining that a change in medication to treat a depressive order, which Lisa was unaware of, had made her volatile and she was sorry. Lisa wasn't buying it. Joanne had been an unpredictable bully for too long. Lisa calmly explained that their partnership was finished, and that she would be in touch to work out a separation agreement. Her relief was instant and overwhelming. For 10 years she had seen Joanne only as a bright, cheerful and generous collaborator, even though her husband had detected problems early on. "Joanne's not who she appears to be," he had cautioned Lisa. "She's all smiles while she's manipulating, but the minute she has you where she wants you, she will show another side."

The last two years of formal partnership had proved him right, Lisa thought. Thank goodness she had not tied herself to a long-term lease. Somewhere in the back of her mind, her husband's words had been like warning bells, urging her not to sign. But still she faced the problem of extricating herself from the current business and setting a new course.

Trusting someone before they have earned it is unwise, but assuming that everyone we meet is untrustworthy is needlessly cynical. So, what's the appropriate strategy? Good BEQ suggests we simply resist forming an opinion about a person's character or personality, until we see how they act over time, and in different circumstances. This won't be easy at first. It requires living with the anxiety of suspending judgment instead of relaxing into a false sense of rapport and trust.

When Success Feels Uncomfortable

Many professionals are most at ease when wrestling, day in and day out, with struggles whose contours are familiar to them. Growth and change might bring rewards, but it also raises troubling feelings and sacrifices.

Success can alter how we relate to ourselves, our personal history, our family, friends, and loved ones. And career progress often demands that we let go of people, places, beliefs, and habits that make up the fabric of our lives. Most successful people will tell you that living up to their potential inevitably demanded that they make difficult sacrifices and relinquish things they cared about.

Staying comfortable, therefore, might dictate that we unconsciously choose a state of being, or set of circumstances, that don't disrupt a status quo we need more than we need the career triumphs we claim to have mapped out for ourselves. Setting ourselves up to fail often occurs subtly, involving self-defeating behavior that defies rational thinking and is hard to spot at first glance.

Ever met someone who has no sooner made it to the top of their profession than they begin behaving seemingly out of character, or so recklessly that they destroy everything they have worked for? Like the newly elevated corporate manager who suddenly starts drinking heavily at lunch, missing deadlines, or becoming unpredictable, until they end up getting fired? If so, you've seen self-destructive behavior, firsthand. And inevitably you've met someone whose unconscious goal was to fail in order to remain stuck in what is emotionally familiar.

Acknowledging destructive acting out can be unnerving, but by recognizing when it happens, we have a fighting chance of clearing it.

Positive Thinking: A Reality Check on a Classic Belief

There is an enduring claim that thinking positively is critical for success in life and work. Think positively, we are told, and you will succeed. And why not? It's obvious that you can't succeed if you think negatively.

But the reality for most of us is that even when we do think positively, we still struggle to achieve our goals, or, we should say, the goals we claim we want to achieve. Ironically, we can easily become negative about thinking positively! "Why should we believe that a positive attitude works when setbacks keep happening and we fail?" we tell ourselves. And then it's even harder to think positively, so we give up on "being positive" and lapse into stale, old thinking patterns.

If positive thinking is a magic bullet, why doesn't it work? The answer is simple but not obvious: Our thinking is almost always contaminated with underlying, self-limiting scripting and rationalizations, which are hard to pin down, and which override our surface attitude, no matter how positive.

If you feel discouraged, and must continually remind yourself to think positively, consider it a clue that you're in the grip of a hidden agenda, which is making you feel miserable and unfulfilled, but which you can't face. Perhaps it's easier to continually command yourself to be positive than to confront counterproductive behavior you might be able to change, if only you would examine it.

If, for example, people don't seem to be responding well to what you're saying, don't blame them. Look inward—openly and honestly. Each time a relationship blows up, instead of relying on a "think positive" mantra, and convincing yourself that the next situation will be better, dig for the truth instead.

Seek honest feedback and, without self-recrimination, ask yourself what you could have done differently in any disappointing situation or setback. Only then do you have a chance of eliminating what is impeding you. Or if you can't identify the underlying cause, at least develop a strategy to work around it—something we will look at later.

People with compulsive behaviors are a good example of what happens when unresolved emotional conflicts drive them. By acting compulsively, or thinking in a rigid or repetitive manner, they are able to relieve, or at least lessen, their upset. Their compulsions, however, often prevent them from relating well to others and prospering. In effect, they manage underlying personal anxieties through their compulsions, but in so doing, they also undermine progress.

BEQ Case Study: In the Grip of Compulsion

Bruce was extremely intelligent. He had worked successfully for several leading management consulting firms, before becoming a partner in a new consulting practice. Now he was one of four strong-willed, highly accomplished men, with four very different approaches to solving problems and getting things done.

Bruce soon discovered that he couldn't handle the noisy leadership meetings and the disagreements and conflicts that were continually at play. He took refuge in being a perfectionist, who spent hours poring over his spreadsheets and proposals, making sure every detail of formatting was correct. "That's not the best use of your time, Bruce," his partners nagged him. "We need you on calls with clients. Let a junior associate do the clean-up on presentations." But Bruce loved losing himself in perfecting his proposals. He sat with partners, meticulously arranging and color coding data, while they tried to get him to focus on thinking through complex strategies, instead of fine tuning PowerPoint presentations.

Truth be told, Bruce could outstrip his colleagues in developing strategy when he focused, but the pressures of his job, caused by interpersonal conflicts, group dynamics, and politics, were too much for him. He retreated into the busywork that soothed him. After two years, his partners gave him his marching orders. His perfectionism was laudable, they explained, but misapplied and costing them revenue. Bruce just couldn't see the wood for the trees. They had brought him in to be a high-level, revenue-generating strategic thinker and not an overpaid PowerPoint jockey.

Getting Comfortable With Discomfort

Getting comfortable with being emotionally uncomfortable is essential in identifying and managing roadblocks that interfere with your progress. Over time, you'll discover that the discomfort you may have always been avoiding is in fact something that, if you sit with it for a while, you can manage. And if you learn to live with any momentary emotional discomfort you are willing to face, you will find that your ability to break through in demanding situations will increase.

CHAPTER 8

Deceptive and Misguided Decision Making

Fairy Tales From Business School

The path for covering up inferior, emotionally driven decisions in companies is greased, because the business community is mostly in lock-step in denying that it happens. Couple this with the fact that business schools and the business community spend scant time on exploring the emotional landscape in business and focus instead on theory and prescriptions. The real shame is that because they do not learn to address the emotional component and strengthen BEQ, many otherwise talented professionals struggle year after year to find formulas for success.

They fail to realize that business success can sometimes be akin to a game of lotto, in which players flourish, more by good luck than by good management, often by simply being in the right place at the right time. Or by falling in with a winning team, in a high-functioning environment that is well organized, with a culture that is geared for success.

The Cover-Up Game

It is not uncommon for business executives to arrange costly office relocations just to make a personal commute easier and then justify the move with some manufactured excuse about it serving the business. Or to schedule costly and unnecessary junkets overseas and bring family members along for a family vacation disguised as a business trip. Others like Nancy hire friends or family over more qualified candidates. Forward-thinking self-dealers toss lucrative contracts to associates for kickbacks or to rack up favors that can be cashed in down the road.

Self-dealing is everywhere and usually papered over or protected with a code of silence. Subordinates might be wary about reporting unethical conduct. Board members look away. Perhaps because they are guilty themselves, or are designated partners in crime. Or perhaps because they are willing to indulge an executive's shady personal agenda in return for promised business results. The message is clear: We consider self-motivated decisions and fiscal abuses as the cost of doing business.

But what happens when self-dealing executives do not get hoped-for results? Colleagues and the board may opt to sweep questionable behavior under the rug. Afterall, they have been complicit in allowing it to go on. Greedy and self-interested executives seldom perform well in the long run. No surprise, since their primary motivation is feathering their own nests, and exploiting a business budget for as many personal goodies as possible.

And yet low characters often roll from one lucrative position into another. Why? Because they look good on paper. Because associates are reluctant to expose the executive's greedy dealings when a new employer calls for a reference. And very often, because such types are shrewd. They understand quid pro quo. They subtly buy the cooperation and silence of those around them as well as entrées into lucrative new job opportunities, after the previous ones crash and burn.

BEQ Case Studies: When Currying Favor Is a Full-Time Job

Stephanie started out in sales. She was great with people and knew how to make prospective buyers comfortable enough to say yes to any deal in record time. She advanced quickly, until she snagged a high-paying position, running a team of account managers at a large international technology firm.

Stephanie was superb at managing the firm's client relationships. She was even better at pressing her personal agenda. Stephanie's focus was always on how to win people over as allies and supporters. Using favors, flattery and leverage, she bought her way into the good graces of everyone she worked with. Stroking others for personal gain filled so much of her day that Stephanie was forced to put a part-time assistant on her company's payroll to get her personal agenda accomplished.

Stephanie collected personal data and important dates in her colleague's lives. Every day, she and her assistant undertook all the tasks needed to make sure every associate was "team Stephanie." They sent associates, subordinates, clients, and bosses alike holiday gifts, thank-you notes, fresh flowers, gift baskets, as well as condolence, graduation, birthday, and even anniversary cards.

Stephanie wrote recommendation letters for the children of associates who were interviewing for work or college. And she drafted glowing references for any colleague who asked. She gave one employee the thrill of a lifetime, by sneaking him a VIP ticket, from a batch purchased for a client event, to see his favorite football team in the play-offs. "Don't say anything," she told another subordinate, "but your name came up on the list of people to be cut in the next round of rightsizing. Don't worry, I'm not going to let that happen." And she made sure others knew when she had backed them for promotions.

Stephanie gave her team time off, gifted spa days, and arranged expensive team building events at luxe locations. She won over even those who were initially lukewarm about her. Few could resist the treats, favors, and compliments she sent their way. And in return, those around her fell over themselves to get Stephanie what she needed. Her employees would step in to do her work, writing the reports or proposals that were central to her role. At performance review time, everyone, even in a 360-degree review, could be counted on to give Stephanie glowing praise. Everyone was fiercely loyal to Stephanie. They performed her duties, covered her mistakes, and were complicit in helping her achieve her career ambitions.

What's the big deal? you might ask. Wasn't Stephanie just being shrewd in knowing how to win people over and influence others? True, but any skill when overused becomes a liability. Stephanie pursued quid pro quo to an extent that was borderline unethical. She created an atmosphere in which coworkers felt indebted to her, and this obscured business-first objectivity and principles. Stephanie created a cozy enclave of self-serving "work family," who sometimes put their own interests before those of the business. They operated primarily based on personal attachments and mutual self-interest.

From Unethical to Criminal

Stephanie's behavior is troubling but relatively benign compared to outright unethical and dishonest business operators, who have characters disorders, such as narcissism or antisocial disorder. Or who are actual criminals.

As the chief technology officer at a Dallas credit platform, Jeb bankrupted the startup company within one year of joining it, by hiring a friend's software development company and blowing the budget on exorbitant developer costs. These included a $10,000 monthly kickback that Jeb's friend paid him out of the fees he billed. Jeb rationalized the pay-off, by telling himself that the fair but moderate CTO salary the startup was paying him was not enough to fund his high-flying lifestyle. He needed the spiff. Jeb's employers were soon out of money and forced to close the company's doors. Colleagues suspected but could not prove that Jeb had been embezzling, as he rolled on to a new assignment that one of his cronies had teed up for him.

The Jebs of the world know how to manipulate others, in ways most of us would never think of, to get what they want for themselves. They have us at a real disadvantage. While we're following what we think are rules of fair play, they're plotting how to use those rules against us. They know full well that most of us want to believe everyone is following the same golden rule book. But, for them, it's all a game. When they cheat, they count on no one else cheating. Hard to believe? Finding such a possibility unsettling could be the very reason that you don't see when it is actually taking place.

BEQ Awareness Tip: What's driving your decision making? The next time you face a business decision, write your considerations down. Then take a moment and ask yourself the following questions:

- Did you find yourself making the safest personal choice instead of the one that best satisfies business interests?
- If so:
  - To what extent are you inclined to cover up this personally motivated decision by rationalizing that it's a plausible business choice?
  - Are you uncomfortable having to cover up personal needs, such as an inclination to avoid risk at all cost?

- Do you feel your progress is limited, because you find yourself unable to take reasonable and well-calculated business risk?
- Do you think your management is limiting you in any manner, or could it be you purposely joined a company that does not encourage employees taking the initiative?

If your answers suggest that objective business interests win out over unproductive personal inclinations, congratulations, you're demonstrating good BEQ.

Coping With Business Unknowns

Business is filled with troubling unknowns that bring unwelcome fears to the surface. When this happens, these fears can lead us into decisions that create undue risk. Here's an example. People working for large companies often speculate endlessly about their work conditions to try to eliminate unknowns. They assess and reassess their job security based on what they hear around the water cooler and on fluctuating corporate circumstances: changing management, updated strategies, shifting market demands, downsizings, restructurings, or mergers.

These obsessive speculators might start looking for a new job, if they fear their company is starting to experience financial problems and a slide into extinction. Once anxiety takes over, reality becomes irrelevant. The only consideration to take center stage is finding what they imagine to be a secure job.

Invariably, the need to be anxiety-free trumps good business judgment, so much so that they may not even take a close enough look at the situation they choose to transition into. Simply finding a new job to relieve current and perhaps misplaced anxiety can become more important than the appropriateness of the new position they ultimately secure.

What's Behind Your Goal Setting?

Were you ever dissatisfied with your business progress? If so, did you feel you'd be happy if you reached your next designated career goal? If you reached that goal, did it satisfy you? Or did you feel empty or disconsolate soon after taking home the prize? If so, did you set another goal and stay obsessively focused on it?

There is nothing wrong with goal setting for the right reasons. In fact, it's a crucial ingredient in career success. But if the hot pursuit of any goal is merely to satisfy restlessness, or to run away from unsettling concerns, instead of wrestling them to the ground, then it's simply a distraction technique—a way to cope with anxiety, to escape the present, or drown out worries about a future that none of us can predict or guarantee.

Worried about outcomes and unknowns, we will often project our fears into the future, catastrophize, or create illusions to avoid facing the fact that we can often do little more than sit tight until prevailing circumstances or players allow us to move forward. For example, have you ever tried to persuade someone to collaborate with you on a project or partnership, and then had to sit back and await their decision? Did you spin your wheels, trying to guess if they would commit to going along with you, feeling good if you thought they would, and fretful if you feared they would pass?

Being preoccupied with trying to assess outcomes we have no control over is futile, and it pulls focus and energy that could be better spent elsewhere. Just accept that you won't know until a decision is made or an outcome decided. Instead of wasting time on fretting and guessing, demonstrate good BEQ and turn your attention to developing new opportunities, while you wait.

This way you'll have a contingency plan to address various *outcomes*. Who knows, an alternate plan may turn out to be better than the original one. For some, though, second or multiple options might be cause for worry, because they create confusion, forcing a stressful decision about which direction is best.

The point is to wait and deal with problems and outcomes, only if and when they occur. Avoid the anxiety of hypotheticals and fears about what has not actually happened yet. Interestingly, a real as opposed to an imagined choice is never as difficult to make as we fear it might be. In fact, when presented with facts in real time, the next step in our decision making process usually becomes obvious.

Keep your head in the present. Don't get ahead of yourself. Avoid needlessly anticipating disappointment, or celebrating success that hasn't manifest, or counting money that isn't in the bank yet. Easy to say, but extremely hard to do. And a hallmark of superior BEQ.

BEQ Awareness Tip: If anticipating outcomes makes you anxious, don't be hard on yourself. It's more important to be clear-eyed enough to acknowledge what you are experiencing than to try to relieve your anxiety or guilt about how you work. Eventually, with practice, all of this will come automatically, and you will have the clarity not to fret about what hasn't happened yet—or to forgive yourself if you do.

What's the bottom line here? Not allowing fear of the unknown to control us—something most of us have a hard time doing. And recognizing that there will always be unknowns in any business situation. The professionals who are able to do this often successfully engage a wide-open career track. Relaxed and ready for anything, they seem better than most at anticipating how others will act, or how situations will turn out.

Do you wonder what they have? Well, invariably they're not too personally conflicted. Low in neuroticism, they are not beset by negative feelings or deterred by criticism. They're realistic, common-sense, and unthreatened by seeing the truth of a situation. They take in a fuller picture, which enables them to gauge more realistic outcomes. And they don't fret over what they can't control. Good BEQ improves our emotional eyesight to aid decision making, not allowing worry to get the better of us.

Fear: The Number One Reason for Ineffective Decisions

Fear derails good decision making and it plagues the workplace, especially in corporate America. Employees slow or block progress day in and day out based on fear: fear of the unknown, fear of a boss, fear of being fired, fear of not meeting business goals, fear of not being accepted, fear of not getting a promotion or raise. Fear of so many things.

Fear often manifests as negativity. Being thought of as negative can make us uncomfortably self-conscious, but being told we lack the courage to face fear head-on can be worse. Whatever the cause, fear is the biggest business hot button, even for those who always appear optimistic.

Accepting the *possibility* that fear could be driving our decisions better prepares us to deal with it constructively. Denying it blocks us from owning up to and effectively dealing with fears that clog progress.

Managing fear can be a real challenge. The next time you're starting to worry, sit down in a quiet place, and see if you can identify what you think may be at least one underlying cause. Acknowledge it, no matter how ridiculous or unrelated it seems. Do this each and every time you start to worry, and you'll begin to see your fears in the proper light, as often emanating from concerns that are irrational, irrelevant, or no longer have a place in your life. Once you understand and master this, your BEQ will increase and your stress level will go down.

Learning to manage fear is critical, because business challenges often make us confront our deepest fears, like losing job or financial security. Interestingly, there are people who enthusiastically attack business obstacles, free of fear. They view problems merely as personal challenges to be conquered. They go forward undeterred, even though they may experience moments of self-doubt. They've learned to live with their fears, or put them in proper perspective. This allows them to cope with uncertainties, and to overcome emotional impediments that cause others to give up.

You can practice these skills until you, too, become like these winners. There's no personal growth, unless we learn how to welcome and solve problems calmly, keeping fear and anxieties under wraps.

CHAPTER 9

Setting an Emotional Frame of Reference

The Why Doesn't Matter

We've touched on how a major stumbling block on the road to success is not taking full responsibility for our own lack of progress. There is little point in looking to blame parents, family, teachers, or other influences and circumstances for burdening you with any hang-ups that might bedevil you. Nor is there any point in self-recrimination. It's best to just ditch the blame game and commit to finding the fastest ways to effect the personal change that powers your progress.

First, accept that it is not always necessary to understand why you are the way you are and do the things you do. What matters most is that you learn to recognize and change the thinking and behavior that does not serve your best interests. There are almost as many theories about why people have specific emotional hang-ups as there are therapists to treat them. But discussing general theories about why we have or hold on to emotional eccentricities is of little value in getting us on the fast track to correcting them.

While we may be in touch with some of the inner conflicts that trip us up, there are many aspects of ourselves which impede progress that we, and even those who know us best, may be oblivious to. Of course, mentors and counselors can be useful in helping us to uncover and confront self-limiting behavior to negotiate the world better, as long as their counsel is rooted in real-world application and efficacy.

But spending ages on analyzing and resolving deep-seated issues is a time sink that we may not be able to afford, as we are tasked with the immediate demands of making a living. We're told by experts in human behavior that resolving ingrained conflicts is very complex and can take years of counseling, with no guarantees. Many people are willing to make the time and financial investment in therapy or coaching. Others feel too overwhelmed by the commitment to even begin and continue to just stumble along.

How then, working alone, can you make headway? One way is by simply learning to observe yourself in the business environment and beyond, becoming exquisitely attentive to how you and those around you function and respond emotionally. Examining your reactions and choices, by looking at yourself unflinchingly, will enable you to develop and experiment with strategies that can help you avoid self-inflicted wounds. And over time, counterproductive habits, including the ones that used to be hidden, will surface and fall away, even if you never entirely figure out why they existed in the first place.

What this book is asking you to do is to rethink how you view the business arena and transact from an emotional perspective. Cultivating street-smarts and BEQ allows you to find simple shortcuts and solutions to any business obstacles you encounter, regardless of what has held you back up until this point.

Keeping It Simple

Even the experts among us often miss the simple solutions. And yet when great solutions do emerge, in any walk of life, have you noticed how so often they are simple or elegant? Does it take a genius to find a simple but profound solution? Most of us think so. But more often than not, this is not the case. The "genius" who sees something that the rest of the world misses is often less mired in conventional thinking and therefore free to see the problem clearly, realistically, in a fresh way, and be open to solving it creatively.

They also don't let conventional thinking or preconceived ideas, or expectations about their chances of success, stop them from trying and persevering. Always maintaining the status quo offers little by way of productive change. Starting something fresh—any new direction—automatically puts us on a path to unforeseen opportunities that we could not have anticipated.

BEQ Case Study: Just Press Cancel

Kevin was naturally ambitious but also seemingly allergic to opportunity. He was an excellent financial and credit analyst and very well respected. Several startups had reached out to tap him for exciting roles in the fintech industry that combined cutting edge technology, with expert credit know-how, to launch next-generation lending platforms. Each time a new job offer dropped into his lap, Kevin felt excited. He longed to escape the narrow function he performed in the cookie cutter cubicle, at the mega bank, where he had worked for eight years.

He would talk over each new offer with his wife, who was very supportive, and explore all the ways an exciting new role would stretch him and make his work life more stimulating and worthwhile. But within a few days, like a balloon slowly losing air, Kevin would feel deflated and gradually talk himself out of the move. Each time he did this, he experienced terrible conflict and disappointment. He knew that he was yearning to move on, but an invisible hand always slammed the door tight shut, as he tried to step out into new pastures.

One night, sleepless with worry, Kevin's mind was racing so much that he suddenly found himself mentally outside himself, watching his own thoughts. He observed a constant stream of doubts, fears, and worries stream through his mind like a mental podcast he was powerless to end. "Stop!" he finally called out. And in that moment, Kevin realized that he could control his thoughts, or at least redirect them. He noticed that when he allowed negative thoughts to spool unchecked, he felt anxious and stressed. When he stopped a negative train of thoughts in its track, he saw how his mood settled and he felt upbeat.

Suddenly awoken to his power over this incessant, internal naysaying, Kevin practiced silently commanding his wayward thinking to cease. Whenever he caught himself "negatizing," as he called it, Kevin would simply say "cancel" to stop the thoughts that were tormenting him and return to the reality of the present moment.

Kevin was the only child of two overprotective and nervous parents. He had trained as a risk manager. His whole orientation was to worry and anticipate problems and then try to mitigate risk. But what was a useful professional skill—continually managing risk—had become a personal liability, often leading him to catastrophize and anticipate the worst outcomes for himself.

"Cancel" became Kevin's secret weapon in stopping the thinking that was doing him in. It was a simple but powerful solution. By repeatedly stopping the negative commentary in his head, Kevin was able to center himself in the present moment to contemplate and make a career move. He calmly weighed the pros and cons of the next new position he was offered. Deciding that it was time to risk indulging his ambition, he reassured himself that he could handle any curve ball a new situation might throw his way.

Clearing Your Mental Deck

People who are rejected, or who encounter obstacles on their first attempt at a goal, can allow themselves to become overwhelmed and give up. If you didn't know how to play golf, would you consider yourself a failure at the game if you scored poorly the first time you ventured onto the green? Of course not. You would acknowledge that it takes experience, knowledge, and practice to hone playing skills.

The same is true for business, yet people rarely pursue business in the same manner as they would a new sport. The process for both, however, is very similar. With calm, confidence, effort and determination, we are able to practice our skills and eventually master each challenge.

That was then and this is now. Avoid using the past as your guide to the future. It's helpful to reflect on the past to gain insight and solidify useful experience. It's a mistake to assume that what worked in the past will work in the future, or that you are locked into outdated attitudes and behavior that are no longer relevant and do not serve you.

Your Awareness Development Situation

Take a few minutes now and see if you can identify a personal trait you find troublesome and which triggers a reaction you're unhappy with. For example, if you cannot carry on a lively conversation at a networking event, do you leave feeling dissatisfied with yourself? How about stumbling over your words when making an important presentation at a business meeting? Or an inability to express yourself as succinctly as you would like? No matter how small, write it in your Development Diary. If you can't identify anything, place a mirror under your nose and see if any mist forms on the mirror.

The Analysis

Let's assume that you were able to identify a disruptive emotional hang-up that plagues you in business—perhaps your worry about being tongue tied or shy; unsociable, long winded, boring, or self-conscious. If so,

- Is this something that you've been frustrated with for a long time?
- Do you feel this is how you are, and you're stuck with it?
- When you think about the issue, are you self-critical?
- Do you feel this conflict is harming your chances for success?
- Do you blame someone in particular for the way you are, in this instance, or just yourself?

Here are a few suggestions:

- Avoid exaggerating the importance of such quirks and using them as an excuse for failure. We all have limitations that we must overcome. And even if we cannot completely correct our deficits, there is no reason why they have to be deal breakers.
- Develop a sense of humor or self-effacing attitude about your quirks rather than being uptight or self-conscious. We all tend to look favorably at colleagues who can joke about shortcomings and maintain a light touch.
- Consider that you are misperceiving your "faults," magnifying them out of all proportion.
- Rest assured that others do not obsess over your imperfections the way you do, so hold them lightly. Laugh them off.
- Accept that using them as an excuse to fail is a cop-out.
- Do *not* signal to enemies that these sore points are ammunition they can use against you.

- Get to what is underneath your fears and any negative self-talk. Perhaps others saddled you with unfair criticism or characterizations when you were younger. Maybe someone unfairly and incorrectly convinced you that you were stupid or boring or inarticulate.
- Work to separate fact from fiction. Reject ancient and misplaced opinions that do not reflect present truths about you, your behavior, and how those around you now perceive and appreciate you.

Constantly clearing your mental deck, fostering a fresh outlook, and adapting your thinking to address current circumstances is an important aspect of BEQ. Some people never update their hair style, their wardrobe, their musical tastes—or their attitudes, self-image, and emotional outlook. Stagnation breeds failure.

To summarize then, when inner tendencies block progress, don't waste your time trying to figure out the cause if it's not readily apparent. That's something you can resolve later, as you move forward. And don't allow yourself to dwell on who you might think put you in the spot you're in or feel guilty about whatever impediments you've held onto. Take full responsibility for being where you are, and getting yourself out of any emotional rut or predicament you find yourself in.

CHAPTER 10

Uncovering Emotional Baggage

Spotting Well-Hidden Emotional Baggage

We bring into adult life unconscious emotional baggage that limits full access to our innate talents. When we're free of these limitations, we do extremely well. When they control us, we pay an emotional, career, and financial price.

While it's off putting to acknowledge when we are not managing our career well, it's often downright alarming to realize that we might be oblivious to how we're manufacturing career problems by unknowingly acting out hidden conflicts.

So, when your career is stalled or lackluster, part of the challenge involves discerning if some unrecognized or well-concealed personal issue might be causing mischief—whether within ourselves, or in someone else, or a combination of both. Clearly, it's unrealistic to believe you could uncover the cause of someone else's unconscious motivations. And it's likewise challenging to believe that, without outside guidance, you can peel back the covers on your own.

So, the real question is: How can you spot what you're doing unconsciously to cause a problem when you have no clue as to what it could be? The key word here is clue.

A Multistep Process

Before we explore the clues that point to unconscious agendas, we should keep in mind that detecting clues is just one step in a multistep process of strengthening BEQ. Once you uncover possible clues, you next need to kickstart a plan of thinking and acting to tackle what you now know is derailing you. And this might require that, at a minimum, you let go of having to know why something is happening and just deal with its outward result or symptom.

Clues, Discomfort, and One More Strategy

Seeing clues to hidden agendas is a real chore at first, and quite taxing, because we unconsciously filter most clues out of our awareness so they don't disrupt us. When you get the hang of clue spotting, however, you'll learn to work with emotional clues as you would with any other business tool.

There is no simple rule of thumb for determining whether a clue exists. Clues are elusive and not always what we might expect them to be, initially appearing as normal reactions to whatever is taking place. For example, how often do we see chronic complaining as a clue to troublesome, underlying inclinations? What about unsettled feelings, restlessness, anxiety, fear, boredom, unhappiness or feelings of inadequacy?

Clues might also surface as provocative actions or statements, such as being late to meetings, or being negative, ill-tempered, and unduly critical or uncooperative. Any of these can be tip-of-the-iceberg indications. As you become comfortable in accepting the oft times stark realities of what is happening within and around you, spotting clues to hidden agendas is something you'll become skilled at doing and grateful for.

Once you have found clues, you may be able to go directly to unearthing, tackling and eliminating the underlying emotional impediments they point to that are confounding you. This, however, is not always possible. But even if you can't knock down a block and root out an issue that trips you, you can end-run it. This can always be done.

As we said, to become skilled at identifying clues, you must be willing to live with the discomfort of facing head on and viewing honestly what is counterproductive within yourself or those around you. And, as you learn to forgive yourself and others for having failings and self-destructive tendencies, and take it in stride, you'll relax and become adept, as part of your everyday routine, at consciously identifying clues to the stubborn habits that hold us all back.

Here's a hypothetical situation to get you thinking about how to end-run an emotional roadblock, the cause of which you can't identify or eliminate.

An Awareness Development Exercise

Assume you're a manager who believes the pinnacle of success is becoming the president of a Fortune 500 company. You desperately want to succeed, but your performance ratings are poor, and your progress slow, despite the countless hours you've spent trying to improve by reading books and taking management courses. You're completely frustrated at this point, because you cannot seem to really get a handle on why you're doing poorly.

Stop for a moment before you read further and see what you think might possibly be a clue to an emotional roadblock in this situation.

The clue is the fact that you have the desire but are unable to get anywhere near the results you want.

Now that you have a clue, you have several options: One is to sink time and money in counseling or coaching, taking a hard look at possible developmental challenges to your progress. Another is to accept the distinct possibility that an unconscious aspect of yourself is setting you up for failure—and then take the responsibility for doing something about it.

Perhaps one overlooked factor is your refusal or inability to see that you are working for an unfair or destructive boss, who is threatened by you and judges you unfairly, while you, instead of solving the problem, do nothing more than complain about how he is holding you back.

If so, you may find, by being honest with yourself, that you have little confidence that you can do well, and that your boss's poor treatment reflects your own low opinion of yourself. Whatever the reason, acknowledge the possibility that you're being self-destructive by continuing in the relationship. And switch your focus to envisioning and pursuing the type of environment, managers, and colleagues you believe would better serve you.

On the road to success, good bosses are better than good jobs. Because no matter how fulfilling work tasks might be, our equilibrium and confidence can be destroyed by a destructive, unpredictable, or undermining superior, if we don't know how to handle them. Whereas good bosses can mentor, groom and generally support our development into a talented, stable, and marketable professional. Convincing yourself that you deserve a supportive boss is often the first step in setting out to find one.

Recognizing, in a situation like this, that you may be indulging self-destructive tendencies, by sticking with a toxic boss, can be a key to setting your creative mind to work, and allow you to honestly re-evaluate assumptions about yourself or your career.

Another consideration might be that, after seriously taking stock, you realize that your stated career goals don't really reflect your changing, hidden, or authentic needs. You may wake up to the fact that the dream of, say, being a top executive, is just an unchallenged habit or placeholder, or a path you set out on to please someone else, or to live up to some old and naïve notion of success.

Confronting ourselves honestly leads us constructively to reshaping career goals, so they fit better. We might experiment with a fresh ambition or role, taking a new management course, exploring truer strengths and passions, even changing careers altogether. The point is to reexamine how you've been thinking—or not thinking and just mindlessly plodding—because it is easier to fall asleep at the wheel of our career than to dig deep and be honest about what we really want and then risk going for it.

Working With Clues

Clues point to buried motivations, alerting you to when you, or someone you know, are creating illusions or false beliefs to cope with what is too difficult to process emotionally.

A good clue is when an associate does or says something that makes no business sense, such as constantly interrupting in meetings, so others are unable to express a different or conflicting opinion. In this scenario, rather than wasting time complaining, or searching to make sense out of it, accept the annoyance and develop a strategy to handle it.

Taking this behavior personally could indicate a blind spot of your own. Instead of believing that the interrupter is rejecting you or your input, instead recognize that typically such people simply want to shut down ideas that upset them. By disrupting the flow of conversation or ideas or opinions, they are able to manage their inner anxious state, refusing to acknowledge those that threaten them, or entertain interactions or attitudes that disrupt them.

We are taught to take people and situations at face value, and not to question the reasons they give for their decisions. Second guessing is considered impolite, even unprofessional, so we ignore the deeper significance of certain attitudes and actions, and miss clues because we hold beliefs that we never think to question. BEQ makes us probing, able to see past superficial explanations, to penetrate hidden motivations and assess situations more clearly.

CHAPTER 11

Honing Business EQ by Spotting Tell-Tale Behaviors

Common Clues to Look for

An important aspect of BEQ is tuning in when your gut tells you something is amiss and using it as a trigger to start clue hunting. The following list is not exhaustive. It's simply a sampling of obvious clues that may surface—and is meant only to kick start your own clue-spotting, en route to unearthing hidden agendas in yourself and others.

Different clues may point to the same or similar underlying cause. Worry and anxiety, for example, are listed as separate clues but are often slightly different expressions of the same underlying problem.

Belief Illusions

Let's call the beliefs and assumptions that we never question, and which may have no basis in fact, *belief illusions*. These are beliefs that we unsuspectingly welcomed with open arms and which may have been imposed on us at a time when we were not in a position to question them. Or they might be faulty beliefs we cling to, in order to avoid unwelcome truths, so that we remain blissfully ignorant or complacent. Any one of them can put and keep us on the wrong track. We're particularly susceptible to belief illusions when we're anxious about the future and want to predict successful outcomes.

Business relies heavily and puts too much stock in long-range and detailed business plans that, in truth, represent only best guesses or hopeful predictions. Plans set the business objectives and intentions that are needed to give all participants a shared vision and solid focus. They also minimize anxieties by framing unknowns in ways that make collaborators comfortable as they proceed.

But instead of acting simply as useful guideposts, while we confront the unforeseen realities of day-to-day business as it is unfolding in real time, business plans too often take on a life of their own. They become set in stone, pointing to glorious market and financial outcomes that may be desirable, but not realistically attainable.

Optimistic revenue predictions sometimes seduce players into suspending their common sense, as they treat their plans as gospel—even as emerging facts suggest otherwise. Misplaced faith in business plans generate belief illusions that lead us astray. No one can predict the future unless, of course, it's failure that we have a hand in!

BEQ Case Study: Tell Us What We Want to Hear

One of the coauthor's first lessons in grasping the illusory nature of business plans was brought home early in his career. He and his partners applied for a working capital loan to expand their consulting business. In their first bank meeting, the loan officer asked where their company would be in five years. The author confessed that the only thing he could verify was what the business had accomplished to date, that they planned to pursue every relevant opportunity, and that they would use fresh capital to meet or exceed their current growth rate. There were so many variables in any business, he pointed out, that no one could know with certainty how the future would pan out. Clearly, this was not what the bank officer wanted to hear. The loan request was turned down.

The following week, the team put together a five-year financial projection and approached another bank. When asked the same question, this time the team simply handed the banker the financial projections, asserting that they full intended to hit the ambitious revenue goals.

The loan was approved and a valuable lesson learned: Even though it's impossible to predict the future, we need, at important junctures, to indulge others in illusions, cleverly disguised as income projections, to make them comfortable so we can get what we need. Failing to recognize that sometimes alleviating anxiety is the priority is a mistake.

BEQ: Key Awareness

Virtually every day, we manage our fears about the future, by creating beliefs that comfort and reassure us that the future looks rosy, and is unfolding as we wish or anticipate. In business we call this "planning." But plans are often just educated guesses or expressed hopes about future events. By contrast, street-smart professionals are fond of quoting former heavyweight boxing champion Mike Tyson, who captured the power and reality of the unforeseen and unpredictable, and the importance of being ready for anything, when he said, "Everyone's got a plan until they get hit in the head."

Clearly, planning is valuable. It gets everyone moving in the same direction. But, forgetting that some plans are often no more than wishful thinking makes us miss seeing when things are not working, and when we must reroute to get what we need. Or budget for failure. Or anticipate looming disaster. Being ready for anything, with the confidence that we can handle it, is a mark of strong BEQ.

Complaining

Complaining is rampant in business, particularly at lunch with coworkers. Once someone starts, it becomes addictive with complaints jumping out of the woodwork. *Complaints can be clues to hidden agendas*, as well as conscious attempts at emotional manipulation. And, for listeners who love to hear complaints about others, it's a clue that they have unresolved, personal conflicts of their own.

When you're listening to complaints, *keep in mind that they seldom reflect the real issue.* And taking someone's words at face value can be misleading. The complainer may be out of touch with what is really bothering him or her, and manufacturing baseless complaints as a cover.

The same goes for your own complaints. If you take them at face value, you can miss what they are really signaling. How often have you complained that someone's feedback was incorrect or unfair, when deep down you knew it was true and pointed to shortcomings you didn't not want to face? It's easier to shoot the messenger than to digest an unwelcome message.

So, when complaints surface, dig deeper to see if they mask hidden issues. If you find yourself chronically complaining about other people, consider the possibility that you are not happy with yourself. When you are able to stop impotently complaining, there is little doubt that you are feeling better about yourself. Think about it.

Pay attention to any nuances in how you react to complaints or negative critiques. For example, you may feel differently about a complaint or harsh feedback, depending on who is delivering it. If it's a friend, you may react one way. If it's a stranger, you may react quite differently. And the difference may depend on how you want to appear to the critic or complainer. Keep reflecting until you figure out why the same complaint makes you feel differently.

A critique about your industry, company, role, or strategy, offered up by a stranger at a networking event, may challenge the image you want to project—your intelligence, position, or prowess in business. If it rattles you, making you feel unsure of yourself or needlessly competitive, you may be more likely to be offended and react defensively.

If, on the other hand, you're relaxed and confident, you're less likely to take any critique or complaining personally, and you might instead see the complainer as a person with problems of their own. Those with low self-esteem often take apparent complaints personally, acting out inappropriately and hobbling themselves.

Handled correctly, complaints clue us in to needed change. Successful salespeople often use complaints to solidify customer relationships. They know a complaint signals that the customer is saying, "I'm unhappy, please do something about it." This is preferable to an unhappy customer who says nothing and takes their business elsewhere. If the salesperson were to become defensive, rather than responsive, they could lose the opportunity to continue a dialogue and establish or maintain a good working relationship. Skillful salespeople don't take complaints personally, and even if they do, they keep their emotions in check.

Anxiety

Many things, real or imagined, make us anxious. Fearful imaginings are a counterproductive way to manage anxiety and often cause it. A classic example of this are people who chronically fear being fired or rejected.

They're quick to misread what is said or happens as a threat to their jobs or popularity, and, all too often, they overreact, saying or doing something that might actually put them at risk.

Anxious people are always in high gear, blocking or rationalizing away upset, while anticipating disaster. Some head for the local bar, others grab a tranquilizer. Some lose their temper at the drop of a hat, others keep themselves frantically busy, and still others masterfully create comforting illusions—all the while relieving only the symptoms and never the causes. There's nothing wrong with ridding ourselves of troublesome symptoms, as long as we acknowledge the possibility that we are papering over cracks, and not actually eliminating the inner conflicts that keep us rattled.

Facing personal limitations, real or imagined, also tends to make us anxious. But when we avoid rigorous and honest self-evaluation, because it unsettles us, we fail to take full advantage of our actual abilities. We have what we have. And vice versa—we lack what we lack. Confronting our limitations in no way diminishes our innate or developed strengths and business abilities. Facing up to where we fall short, and accepting the way we are, or the way we think we are, frees us to realistically tackle shortcomings, make improvements, and move forward.

Stop fretting over meaningless competition. For example, constantly trying to flex and assert how smart you are, in relation to others in your professional sphere, is a useless distraction, but a common one, nevertheless. First of all, there is no way to reliably measure this. And second, a preoccupation with intelligence as a be-all, end-all measure of excellence typically hinders more than helps.

If you're always on a quest to show yourself as the smartest person around as a way to stand out or succeed, you may have been raised by adults and teachers who neglected to help you assess and leverage the full complement of abilities you bring to your work life. High BEQ professionals know how to combine strengths and even mediocre abilities into a unique talent stack they leverage to attack challenges and succeed. Most importantly, they are authentic in recognizing where their weakness and limitations lie, and don't need to project abilities and smarts they don't have, simply to satisfy some comforting self-image. They are committed to progress and results not to ego and appearances.

When you are anxious in a business situation, don't let all the anxiety go to waste! Make a note of what you're experiencing, and use it as a clue to unearth more self-awareness. In time, when the situation has played itself out, revisit what you captured or wrote down, to determine if what you suspected was causing your anxieties turned out to be accurate. By completing this exercise each time, you're overtaken by work-related anxiety, you'll eventually see that most of your concerns are the product of an overactive imagination or unrealistic expectations. Or, if there is some truth to your concerns, you'll learn to accept it and work around it.

Negative Thinking

Negative thinking is a massive clue to unresolved conflict, fearfulness, or lack of self-awareness. What's interesting about negative thinkers is that they continually predict what can go wrong, while seldom anticipating what might go right. Unfortunately, most negative thinkers rarely reach their full potential, even though they sometimes have a small measure of success by gravitating to advisory roles. What they fail to see, along with those who foolishly listen to their advice, is that their own marginal track record disqualifies them from making good business assessments and giving reliable counsel.

In the face of business uncertainty, negative thinking seeks to eliminate uncomfortable risk. When risk-takers forge ahead and run into problems, the naysayers who cautioned them against action look brilliant. The "If you had only listened to me" statement works every time! For negative people, it's better to fail by not trying than to risk failing. If you get upset when you hear negative takes on a situation, use this as a clue to hidden negativity within yourself. Very often, negative people make us uncomfortable, because their negativity makes us aware of our own.

Curiously, negative people are often fearful of knowing they're negative. They go to great lengths to convince everyone, including themselves, that they're just being pragmatic or realistic. Ever met someone who confessed to wanting something and, in the very next breath, lamented that they probably wouldn't get it? Did they try to cover their pessimism with claims that they were just being realistic? The next time someone reacts negatively to something you say, point out to them that they seem quite negative. Use the word "negative" and then stand back and listen to the cover-up.

Some negative thinkers cleverly avoid confronting this shortcoming, by not taking responsibility for their negative decisions or inaction. Think about associates who always consult a spouse about exciting new business opportunities that might involve some risk, only to have the spouse "talk them out of it"? This is a classic way to shift blame to another for a decision we don't want to own. By getting a partner to voice our fears and hold us back, we have an excuse to turn away from risky but possibly rewarding situations, all the while acting annoyed with them for "convincing" us not to take the leap.

If we are really honest with ourselves, we might see that we subtly set our partner up to be alarmed about the proposed situation, by how we lay it out or describe it. Steering them toward caution and "no" instead of a full-throated "Yes, I think you should go for it." Without acknowledging it, we make others the fall guy. We point to a trusted partner or advisor and claim "It was all his fault that I missed a real opportunity."

Embarrassment

Feeling chronically or unnecessarily embarrassed tells you that you are not dealing with unexamined tendencies. If you live in fear of making embarrassing mistakes or doing or saying something foolish, such preoccupations can create stress, which in turn interferes with your ability to function at your best. Under stress, your measurable IQ drops, and you're less likely to think clearly.

We all make mistakes, doing or saying ill-considered things from time to time. It's a fact of life. If you have minimal underlying or unresolved issues, you may feel momentarily mortified by your embarrassing behavior but should be able to put such incidents into proper perspective quickly and move forward. Dwelling on personal embarrassment and blowing it up into a feeling of humiliation or shame that trips you up or inhibits you is clearly a clue that you're undermining yourself.

When you feel embarrassed, investigate until you uncover why, instead of just brushing it off. Sometimes it's not your own behavior but an innocuous comment from someone else that makes you feel self-conscious, embarrassed, or that triggers an old feeling or belief about yourself that should no longer have a valid place in your life. As with other clues, use embarrassment as a way to look within at something you need to eliminate, resolve, or learn to work around.

The same holds true when observing others. Be alert to how an associate's embarrassment could get in your way. Easily embarrassed people, to save face, sometimes get rigidly locked into positions. They might have a cultural, familial, or personal embarrassment around driving a hard bargain, when negotiating for goods and services, either in a work or home setting. This can result in overpaying, often massively, to avoid being seen as cheap or pushy.

Called upon to say no, speak forthrightly, or be decisive, colleagues may instead be overtaken by embarrassment. Early conditioning has taught them not to favor honesty or to act resolutely in their own or your best interests. Face-saving cultures often prize self-sacrifice or people-pleasing over acceptable and straight-forward business transacting.

Being Critical

Those who constantly criticize others are often engaged in obsessively criticizing themselves. Pay attention if you find yourself being routinely critical or focused on criticizing a particular person or type of person. Colleagues who constantly criticize everyone around them are providing valuable insight into their emotional makeup, particularly if the criticism is unfair or unwarranted. The person may have a low opinion of themselves and be engaged in constant self-judging. Wasting time, by trying to understand why they do this, is a useless exercise and a clue to an unhelpful attitude.

In dealing with a relentless critic, your sole objective should be to develop a realistic approach to eliminate or effectively manage what is happening. If your boss is unfairly critical of you, the obvious answer is to look for another job or transfer. Or work to be absolutely impervious to the criticism, and see the position only as a necessary stepping-stone toward a better situation, versus being trapped in a toxic environment that you allow to define your worth. Meanwhile, if a member of your work team can't stop knocking every new idea, get them off the team, so the criticism does not infect others, kill team spirit, and inhibit progress.

Job Fantasies

Constantly fantasizing about aspects of your job or career that you'd like change, but feel you cannot, can be a clue that you unknowingly are avoiding making necessary changes. Maybe you are only too happy to blame circumstances and others for your stalled career, while you settle into harboring unproductive fantasies, instead of breaking down your career challenge into pieces you can realistically tackle one at a time.

And if you select partners who likewise engage in chronic fantasizing and wishful thinking about business and career, see this for what it is: an avoidance technique that keeps culprits stuck in ineffectual ruminating, instead of taking small, manageable but meaningful steps forward.

Dreamers and big talkers often team up, secure in the understanding that the plans they hatch together will never go anywhere. If a partnership with your favorite collaborator always fizzles, after numerous hours spent on planning and false starts, consider that you need to make a switch and seek a partner with a bias to action, who might prod you into meaningful activity, instead of allowing you to daydream on the sidelines.

Frustration and Giving Up

Even with the best planning and resources, things go wrong. We fail. And we inevitably become frustrated. Plenty push ahead, but many give up. Those who quit lose. So, if you're frustrated and want to give up, grit your teeth and change your outlook. Quitting because you're frustrated is a clue to low BEQ and an unrealistic view about what it takes to succeed. Perhaps you are underestimating the importance of perseverance.

Instead of assuming that your idea is a dud, or that you don't have what it takes, remember that if achieving success were easy then few would fail. So, give your plan more time to take root and flourish. The dilettante chops and changes, flitting from one scheme to another to avoid the frustration of getting a venture off the ground. Of course, stubbornly sticking with a plan, long after there is every indication that it is destined to fail, is also deluded. But restlessness that prevents us from staying the course is proof positive that we're not willing to develop the maturity and BEQ to accept the time it takes to turn a good idea into solid reality.

Frustration can be self-manufactured—an excuse to throw in the towel. If you've ever set a personal goal with an aggressive deadline and felt like a failure because the deadline came and went, while progress eluded you, you're a victim of personal self-sabotage that needs addressing. Setting an ambitious schedule is fine, but you must consider rationally why you missed it. If it is due to uncontrollable factors, such as changes in the economy or market demand, or your own unrealistic expectations, and you still feel like you failed, then your feelings are unwarranted and counterproductive. Similarly, if you're collaborating with others who express chronic frustration, make sure it doesn't indicate that they have an immature and unrealistic outlook.

Depression

Depression can point to many psychological issues far too complex to address here. Some are serious and others are not. It may simply occur due to transient circumstances, or be the result of momentary fatigue or disappointment. But depression may also surface when something has touched a personal sensitivity too painful to acknowledge. Whatever the cause, depression is something that should not be ignored. And if it's prolonged, getting professional help is essential, particularly if it's chronic.

Explore depression as a clue to an underlying emotional obstacle that is stifling you. For example, if you enter a prolonged depression, because you didn't get an expected raise or promotion, it may signal an underlying and persistent feeling of low self-worth, which will erode your well-being.

Use depression as a trigger to explore buried conflicts. If it's not severe, and you can sit with it, rather than frantically trying to distract yourself, chances are that contributory causes will surface, including unrealistic and ingrained beliefs or conditioning, as well as submerged anger and frustration. If so, you have the opportunity to sort through and discard what is no longer valid. A great benefit to cultivating this level of personal awareness and insight is that it leads to clarity about what is creating unhappiness, depression, or failure, so you can better orient yourself and ground yourself in healthy thinking.

Worry

People worry when they fear outcomes that seem bad from their perspective. Worry is natural but not when it's chronic. The act of worrying robs you of the moment, saps your energy, and fills your mind with clutter that blocks clear thinking and your ability to use your talents to the fullest. Worry is often a good clue to ancient, unchallenged, or hidden beliefs that need reworking or reframing.

If you don't fully appreciate how worrying distracts or clogs the mind, pay attention the next time you talk to someone who is in the throes of worry. Check if they are really listening to you. Are they resisting or trashing constructive suggestions? Are their eyes darting back and forth or glazed over? Their mind is so filled with static that they can barely process anything you say.

Difficulty in Listening

People who have difficulty staying present and paying attention limit their business potential. When someone is unable to listen, assuming it's not a legitimate learning disability, it's often because they're struggling to keep at bay worries or unwelcome feelings about themselves, others, or their present situation, such as fear that they will look foolish or be unable to perform. And their struggle may go off the charts when they're talking to a boss or someone they think is smarter or superior in some way.

Problem listeners respond in a variety of ways to cover up their inattentiveness. Some are defensive and others avoid dialogue that reveal they can't listen by, for example, controlling the conversation. Not hearing other points of view is preferable to hearing them and then shutting down, feeling lost, or looking stupid. So consumed with personal fears or conflicts, they rarely realize their inability to follow the conversation is caused by an emotional block, not by a lack of intelligence. Some problem listeners learn to cope by taking notes. This may appear odd at times, but it's better than looking or feeling incompetent.

An inability to pay attention is yet another clue to hidden conflicts that need addressing, with personal effort or professional support, before they become a major hurdle.

Avoiding Pressure

Constantly trying to avoid "pressure" suggests you might be running away from inner turmoil. The feeling of pressure is often internally generated, of our own making, and not arising from external sources. We often can't determine the true source of our stress or pressure. Is it generated from inner experiences or outer circumstances, or a combination of both? It's important to unpack where the sensation of pressure we feel is originating, so we can work on reducing it.

Regardless of rank, whether a corporate CEO or a data entry clerk, internal stressors are always at play and generating pressure, albeit for different reasons. No matter its cause, persistent and unresolved internal stress hampers the ability to process information effectively and perform.

Do you find yourself running away from disquieting feelings? Do you sometimes avoid healthy challenges or stretching in your career, claiming that it creates too much "pressure"? Treat this as another clue. Sit with and explore your inner discomfort. See what surfaces. Instead of running from thoughts that make you uneasy, explore them, capturing them on paper. Be on the lookout for similar tell-tale clues among your colleagues. Build your BEQ to actually develop strategies to address this in yourself and others. Don't let internal pressure that you can easily learn to diffuse keep you sidelined instead of engaged and growing.

Frantic Activity or Busy Work

Remember Bruce from our earlier case study, who engaged in busy work, perfecting presentations as a way to avoid facing and resolving conflicts with his partners? When we engage in mindless or frantic activities, it often flags one more attempt to escape free-floating anxiety, arising from misguided feelings and fears that would evaporate if we stared them down. Busy work distracts us and blocks anxiety from surfacing, much like turning the volume up high on a radio creates a distraction. But it also squanders time we could better invest in more worthwhile efforts.

Again, when you feel the need to run away mentally, pay attention to your thoughts. Perhaps there are current circumstances or decisions you find difficult to face. Or maybe there is a deep-seated but vague fear that you have been unable pinpoint, so you have created distractions to drown it out.

High BEQ bestows on us the benefit of being self-aware, and willing to stay in touch with our inner thoughts and feelings, so we can intelligently process what's going on around and within us. From moment to moment, we are willing to examine and tackle what is bothering us about ourselves or others, and to formulate a rational approach to dealing with it versus simply ignoring or papering over.

Excessive Drinking or Drugs

An overreliance on alcohol or other substances—enough said. This is a clue that almost everyone recognizes as indicating an inability to cope. Some people rationalize their drinking or drug use as manageable or desirable, which is often massively self-deluded and destructive.

If this describes you, getting professional help is the only course of action. If it's someone you're working with who cannot, for whatever reasons, get professional help, it's time to change the relationship. It cannot be managed. And any belief that you can manage it suggests you harbor naïve and unrealistic attitudes.

Procrastination

It's the rare person who does not procrastinate from time to time. Being an adult means facing a daily barrage of responsibilities and tasks that require self-discipline, structure, and hard work to manage. The more we want from our lives and careers, the more responsibility we must take on. Chronic and crippling procrastination is often a clue, not that a person is not diligent or hard working, but that deep-seated conflicts or prolonged stress have shut down their ability to perform.

Sometimes we push ourselves too hard and burn out, rendering ourselves incapable of maintaining the daily grind. At other times, our confidence and optimism are so dented that we are reluctant to keep going in the face of disappointment, so we give up. Fear of failure, disillusionment with our chosen path, a sense of being overwhelmed and anxious—all of this can contribute to habitual procrastination that burns daylight and robs us of productivity and a sense of accomplishment.

Much ink has been spilled on how to short circuit procrastination:

- Perhaps it is a sign of a life that is out of balance and needs to be reordered.
- It may signal early developmental deficits in our formative years, when we lacked adults to provide us with structure, good habits, and healthy self-discipline.
- We may be overwhelmed and need guidance on how to break complex tasks down into manageable pieces.
- We may require cheer leaders to kickstart our confidence and drown out an inner critic that says we are destined to fail, so there is no point in trying.

Regardless of why procrastination haunts you, if it does, it's imperative that you tackle it with self-help, coaching, or with a trust circle of friends who are willing to support you. Procrastination is an emotional weed that left to spread can take over our mental space, waste our working day, choke our ambition, and stymie important goals. People often procrastinate and then beat themselves up for wasting time, which further undermines their efforts, leading them to procrastinate further, in a vicious and self-defeating cycle. Don't delay. Stop procrastination in its tracks.

And the Clues Go On

Again, this is not an exhaustive list of clues. But it will put you on the right track to recognizing others that signal you should attend to thought and feeling patterns, in yourself and others that impede progress, and which you can manage with improved BEQ.

As you open up to the possibility of searching for clues that point to self-deception, you will become more and more adept at understanding how your mind works in shutting out unwelcome awareness and realities.

Don't concern yourself with validating all clues beyond all doubt; that in itself is a distraction. Just be on the lookout for clues, and see them as signposts to roadblocks that you can clear away. And remember that most people have blocks, so there is no reason to be unduly self-critical.

BEQ Case Study: When Complaining Is a Habit

Emma was a likeable, creative, experienced marketing manager, who joined a successful recruiting firm that was ready to take business to the next level. Its CEO, Ted, was excited, to hire a professional with such great marketing ideas to be part of the management team that he was beefing up with four new hires. But three months in, although Emma was making progress in designing effective new campaigns, Ted was frayed from her constant complaining.

At least once a day, she stopped by his office to subtly tell tales on a coworker, complain about a vendor, or lament a problem with some project or other. Ted found himself continually trying to bolster Emma and troubleshoot her problems. Pretty soon he was getting feedback from the rest of the team that Emma's constant complaining was off putting and undermining cohesion and team spirit.

Ted turned to his colleague Marion, who was an experienced development coach, to ask if she could pinch hit and get Emma on track. Marion met with the team to get a full picture of the problem and wasted no time in giving Emma forthright guidance: "Emma, you have to stop telling people what you don't like, what you don't want, what bothers you, and what is wrong with them in every situation," Marion said.

> And instead, start telling colleagues clearly and politely what you do want or expect. Instead of complaining that Jim cuts the printer's checks late, ask him if you can please have the check within three days of requesting it. Don't tell Sue she screwed up by ordering the wrong gift bags. Just ask politely if she can exchange them for the correct ones. Don't go to Ted with a problem unless you have thought through a potential solution.

Emma took the advice to heart, but she was stunned to realize how difficult it was, over the coming months, to make the proposed changes to her attitude and behavior. To her dismay, she realized that she derived emotional satisfaction from complaining. Reorienting herself and reframing her communication felt somehow upsetting, but she knew her job was on the line if she didn't do it. She worked diligently to make changes, until one day, she felt a sudden sense of well-being and accomplishment, realizing that her colleagues were relating to her so much better, and that work ran so much more smoothly.

It wasn't until months later that Emma was thunderstruck with an awareness that seemed so obvious but had completely eluded her: Emma's mother was a chronic complainer and nag. Throughout her childhood, Emma had listened to her mother, on an endless loop, spell out everything that was wrong with the people, places, and things around her. And she had watched her father bend over backward to accommodate his wife.

Emma had internalized the lesson: to get what you want, you point out problems and complain, instead of figuring out a solution or asking for what you do want. Being a complainer, Emma saw, put you on the sidelines of the game, shouting criticism at the other players. Being responsible for finding solutions, and clear in articulating needs, made you a team player, contributing to the win, or at least not adding to the problem.

CHAPTER 12

Integrating the Basics

Got the Clues, Now What?

We've discussed how looking for clues can tune us into behaviors that hinder us, prompting us to find solutions. With increasing BEQ, we deal more effectively with reality. We become skilled in dissolving illusions, dispensing with wishful thinking, and acting in a more perceptive, pragmatic, and realistic fashion. This pays dividend across the board, within our personal, professional, and social lives.

Getting comfortable with a more accurate view of reality, you'll see individual behavior patterns you never noticed before and grow to understand attitudes and actions that previously made no sense to you. It will dawn on you that all of these troublesome behavior patterns are giant clues staring you smack in the face, and pointing to blind spots and blocks that you can clear. Now, using these clues, you'll be able to gain the insights necessary to overcome obstacles that you and others put up.

Your ultimate objective in spotting clues is to use them in developing strategies that empower you, without emotionally crushing the well-meaning players around you—the ones who unintentionally get in your way, as well as the saboteurs who deliberately undermine you.

As we said, there is no one-size-fits-all answer for any given situation-–there are too many subtle variables. Developing effective strategies involves trial and error. But your new-found clarity will allow you to make progress, and to maintain your equilibrium, as you assess situations more accurately, without emotionally overreacting to them.

People Are Complicated

Next, we continue to methodically unblock ourselves, by investigating how the troublesome people we often invite into our lives offer a trail of yet more clues. Their destructive emotional characteristics and behavior profile can point to places in us that are emotionally stunted.

If you fail to spot how you are attracted to negative, unhealthy, limited, dishonest, blame-shifting, or grievance-seeking people, as well as other disruptive types, this is a solid clue that, unconsciously, you have chosen to hold yourself back, without understanding or accepting the responsibility for doing so. It's time to be brutally honest about how you may be ignoring, misunderstanding, or rationalizing the behavior of problem people around you.

Getting Real With Some Everyday Stereotypes

Let's look at a few of the personality types that we commonly encounter in business, as well as strategies for dealing with them. Again, these hypothetical types are meant only to stimulate your awareness into seeing patterns of challenging behavior. We're zeroing in on specific traits that are more readily identifiable in the business environment.

- Learn to spot emotional issues associated with various personality traits, styles, and mannerisms.
- Look beyond the surface to unpack why you may be unconsciously allowing others to impede your progress.
- See handling or avoiding problem people like the process of learning to drive. You do not have to know the intricacies of how a car engine operates to become a good driver.

One more important point to keep in mind: Although there's no doubt that you will encounter ruthless or sociopathic people or downright criminals in business, most problem people don't fall into these categories. They're often just controlled by defensiveness, or survival and anxiety-based needs that make them hard to deal with. Again, don't waste time mulling over why someone behaves in a troublesome fashion—that in itself is just an excuse to stall instead of taking beneficial action.

Mr. Big Time

Mr. Big Time is smooth-talking and bombastic with a massive ego, and represents a classic business stereotype. He's emotionally complex with many hidden personal needs and agendas that can create big business headaches for those around him.

Mr. Big Time is a master at office politics, knowing instinctively when and how to seemingly befriend people and move them all over the chessboard to suit his needs. He addresses everyone by their first name, asks about their family, and always has a ready smile. When dealing with him, never forget that his business goals directly reflect his inner needs first, and the needs of others, as well as the business he is involved with, come, at best, a distant second (assuming he even cares or can process the needs of anyone other than himself.)

The Mr. Big Times have a real advantage. And they know it. While we're following the rules of fair play, they're plotting ways to use those rules against us. In fact, they know we'll act in good faith and stick to the rules of fair play even when we're being cheated. They count on us bending over backward to explain away their shady behavior when we glimpse it, because they know that most of us look for the good in others.

There are no rules for the Mr. Bigs. Business is a game they know they can win by maneuvering, while others look away or fail to see the obvious. Even if you catch them red-handed, they'll look you straight in the eye and deny any wrongdoing, gaslighting you until you doubt that what you saw with your own two eyes actually happened. Or they might laugh, slap you on the back, and humbly ask for your forgiveness, promising never to transgress again. And if you give them a second chance, they'll figure out a clever way to create or repeat whatever deception benefits them.

When involved with a Mr. Big Time, it can take years to catch on to what's happening, if ever, particularly if you are not self-confident or experienced in business. These characters know how to manipulate us in ways we've never dreamed of—and certainly never learned about in business school. For them, a key to their disarming style is their big, fake smile, and forced bonhomie that sucks most people in. But their smiling, upbeat manner hides the fact that they always have their hand in your pocket, grabbing whatever is for the taking; all the while telling you how great you are, and how they're here to help you. We often fall for their charm, simply because they can be flat-out engaging and fun to be around. Secretly, they feel superior and believe they can talk their way out of any situation that shows they have their hand in the "till". And very often they can.

Your Strategy: Learning a Process

If you sense someone is a Mr. Big Time, but are confused because he seems generous or supportive, trust your gut. Over time, you'll find it doesn't matter if you're right, as long as you're making progress. And that is the litmus test—progress.

In developing a strategy to handle a Mr. Big Time or any other obstructionist in your life, you must be able to take a hard look at yourself. And that means honestly making an effort to acknowledge how certain characters are manipulating your reactions or affecting your performance. Alternatively, you may be mischaracterizing another, and unfairly blaming them for problems that you create. In either case, the roadblock is real, but your strategies, for obvious reasons, will be different.

Do a mental scan of all the people you are involved with for work. If you think you have a Mr. Big Time disrupting your business life, figuring out how to get from point A to point B, in a way he never sees coming, is the goal. Here are some thoughts to consider:

- Never for a moment doubt that Mr. Big is operating at all times for his own gain—as uncomfortable as this realization is.

- All that matters is what you proactively do to end-run any real or, yes, even imagined roadblocks he has created.

- Don't waste time trying to figure out why he is the way he is—you'll never know. Doing so will prevent you from seeing all the clues right in front of you that will enable you to bypass him.

- Never forget that taking care of your own best interests, when done correctly, will not harm him, but simply prevent him from using you.

- Trying to have an open and reasonable discussion with a Mr. Big Time is a waste of time. It only gives him more ammunition to work you over in ways that you don't see.

- If you have a conversation with Mr. Big Time about how he is being unfair to you, and he says you have a good point, don't trust his response.

- Use the same tactics on him that he uses on you—he'll likely be a sucker for them. Flash the *big* smile and slap him on the back if you can get away with it. And above all, keep your feelings to yourself.

Ms. Back Stabber

Often a passive-aggressive personality, Ms. Back Stabber is also well-known in business circles. If you run into a Ms. Back Stabber, we suggest you arm yourself by reading up on passive-aggressive personalities. There's a lot to learn, because there's a lot to contend with. In a nutshell, this personality type is one of the most confusing, acting out their anger or aggression literally and figuratively behind your back.

While these folks can be congenial and quite outwardly agreeable, the Ms. Back Stabbers are true snakes, hiding in the corporate weeds. If you threaten them, real or imagined, they will become covert, waiting to strike and run before you know what happened. You'll never see directly what a Ms. Back Stabber has done to sabotage you. Any anger or resentment they feel is expressed through covert behavior, rather than through forthright dialogue or action.

For example, if you ask them to perform some task they don't like, they'll agree, but will then procrastinate, forget to do the task, constantly make excuses, or simply do a lousy job. If you disagree with anything they say in a meeting, they may never confront you, and instead run to your boss to plead their case and undermine yours. Chances are good, when this happens, that your back stabber worked their agenda undercover with the boss, giving you a solid clue to their personality type. Needless to say, this type of behavior can create havoc at work.

Some of these personality types can be even more deceiving, appearing meek or a bit shy in casual meetings. At first blush, you might consider them completely harmless. But, be alert. They are masters at company politics, often rising to senior positions by killing off everyone who is, or who they perceive is, endangering their progress. Typically, they achieve this with brilliant and strategic political backstabbing. So, when that fast-rising, easy going, nonthreatening person with the soft and welcoming smile *first* undermines you, be particularly alert for indications that could signal a down-and-dirty passive-aggressive personality.

Back-stabbers love to subtly provoke you, so you'll react poorly in front of others and look unprofessional. This might include actions they've taken behind your back, which are leaked to you by one of their cohorts. There may be some stunt you're sure they pulled, but find hard to prove, that sets you up to look bad.

If your tendency is to act out emotionally, use this as a clue to addressing an important blind spot. When you don't respond strategically, you easily fall into traps set up by passive-aggressive coworkers or associates. So whenever you have an impulse to react to what is unfair, be careful.

Your Strategy: Continuing to Learn a Process

At this stage, focus on continuing to get familiar with the process, rather than on trying to definitely assess a personality disorder or eccentricity. Again, there's no definitive answer for this situation. So, with that in mind, here's a good threshold strategy to consider if you encounter a passive-aggressive personality:

- DON'T react emotionally. Saying anything that is angry or aggressive to Ms. Back Stabber directly and openly shows her that she has hit your hot button—one she will keep pushing in a variety of ways until you self-destruct.
- Develop a game plan to end-run her behavior or diffuse her ability to disrupt your progress. And, for this, if you suspect you're dealing with a passive-aggressive personality, you'll need to do some solid homework on this personality type.
- Because they can be so disruptive in business, your only solution may be to cut off all dealings with them.

Mr. Negative

We've already said a great deal about negative coworkers who toil overtime to block their own progress and the progress of anyone who'll listen to them. Negative attitudes are a primary reason that businesses stall or fail. If you find you're very negative or are drawn to, or unduly influenced by, negative people, this might be a difficult challenge to overcome. And, if, after you become aware of it, the challenge persists, it may require professional guidance to resolve.

Sometimes hard to spot, negative people hide in plain sight. They often seem to be consumed with getting ahead, so it seems illogical to see them as self-destructive. In fact, they delude themselves with their focus on achieving, never realizing how they're unconsciously stymying progress. They are often in career overdrive—going downhill.

Negative types often derail their audience by implying that the best decisions present no risk of unfavorable outcomes. Nothing could be further from the truth, a fact that far too many businesspeople fail to realize. Most of the decisions we make, perfect and imperfect, help us to advance. When you run into a wall, it is simply an invitation to reroute, as you proceed on your path to success. High BEQ professionals are decisive, always moving forward, with a bias to taking action and creating momentum.

Those who don't want to own up to their own negativity hide it by surreptitiously hiring naysayers as advisors, so they can put off coming to terms with their own need to avoid risk and blame it on others instead. So, for unconsciously negative people, openly negative coworkers perform a real service: They hand out ready excuses for steering clear of decisions and actions that might cause fear and anxiety. In effect, it's a guiltless way out of avoiding inevitable business risks. Never forget, a negative person's sole agenda is to ensure they stay in their comfort zone—often a zone of failure. And, if they have a hand in it, those around them will, too.

Your Strategy: Keep Investing in Your Process

Dealing with the negativity is a fact of life. If you think you or someone around you is negative, here are a few threshold suggestions to work with:

- If at all possible, avoid engaging or forming close relationships, personal or business, with negative people.
- Accept that any failure to avoid negative types is a clue to your own negativity. And if you suspect you are negative, start to accept the responsibility for determining why.

- *Don't* deny the possibility that you have a negative tendency
  if you're influenced by negative people or form relationships
  with them. This will help you put into perspective something
  that you need to resolve.
- *Don't* blame others for throwing cold water on your ideas
  or goals.
- If you tend to be slightly negative, avoid making decisions
  when you're tired or your personal resources are otherwise
  low.
- Never forget that even if you're a generally positive, upbeat
  person, constantly having naysayers around will contaminate
  your thoughts and hamper your abilities.
- Always develop a game plan to end-run someone's negative
  attitude so it does not disrupt your progress. That game plan
  may simply be to avoid discussing your thoughts and goals
  with a nearby Mr. Negative.

BEQ Case Study: Shut Out With a Smile

Tina was an excellent freelance project manager who had worked with
Simon at his previous company, before he tapped her to undertake contract work, managing projects at the media firm where he had recently
landed. Tina was meticulously organized and detailed. She brought order
to chaotic projects and workflows, earning rave reviews from Simon's boss
and the rest of his team. Whenever a new project needed an expert to
keep it moving, Tina was the go-to person.

Tina was always sure to let Simon know how much she appreciated
his sponsorship, checking in with him regularly for work opportunities.
Not long after she had inquired with Simon about any upcoming projects
and learned there was none, Tina had lunch with Simon's coworker. She
told Tina that the team was so disappointed when Simon had recently
announced that Tina was not available to manage their current project.
The replacement hire was far less effective Tina's lunch date confessed.

Tina was stunned. She had specifically told Simon that she was free to
work and had believed him when he apologetically claimed that he had
no current needs. Truth was, he had hired someone else, after deliberately
misleading his team about Tina's availability.

Tina knew the knock on Simon was that he managed up—always wanting to look good to his superiors and craving all the credit for any team successes. And while he was a decent manager, he did not groom his team for promotions, nor allow them exposure to senior management, resenting when they, and not he, were praised.

Tina understood that her work had attracted too much positive attention. Simon, she saw, would rather hire an inferior replacement than tolerate her enjoying a high-profile and universal praise, thanks to her excellent performance. Simon was a passive-aggressive sneak, who had smiled in Tina's face and then sabotaged her, when she believed he was operating in good faith and she could trust him.

And There Are Many, Many More

This chapter identifies just a few of the troublesome personality types that are prevalent in business to get you thinking about character traits or patterns of behavior that mark the people you encounter. All of us are, of course, unique, but destructive behavior tends to follow the same patterns, showing up in similar ways from person to person.

BEQ prompts you to build your own street-smart inventory of troublesome types and spot the clues that tell you which one you are up against. This will make you aware of what to expect and how to respond to various characters who deploy disruptive moves.

CHAPTER 13

Negotiating

Setting the Stage

Without a doubt, business or career negotiations can be very stressful, even for seasoned deal makers. If you're someone who doesn't like to appear difficult, to make others uncomfortable, or to ruffle feathers, you likely won't be able to negotiate the best deal, or even the one you were hoping for or need. So, step one in becoming a good negotiator is to be honest with yourself about any and everything that makes you uneasy, when it comes to negotiating any type of business deal or working relationship.

And remember, negotiating is not merely about obvious financial transactions or contracts. More broadly, it is how you manage your interests to survive and succeed in business in general. So, whether it's getting others to accept your ideas, or getting the conditions you want in a contract, you are always negotiating.

Overly agreeable professionals have trouble making demands and asking for compromises and concessions. Any time you're negotiating for a new job, a working arrangement, a contract, or a purchase agreement, start by capturing on paper, from every recess of your brain, all of the worries, concerns, and anxious self-talk that surface. Be honest with yourself. If your general concern is about losing a deal or upsetting someone, those feelings will unconsciously put you in a one-down position, and you may not get what you reasonably need. Additionally, if you feel the need to look smart, hard-nosed, successful, or are simply determined to win every point you make, chances are that this, too, will deep six your chances for achieving a good result.

Identifying What's Really at Stake

The process of negotiation dredges up many feelings, including those buried way down deep. People pleasers, or the overly agreeable, tend to negotiate poorly. This can leave them feeling short changed and plagued with unconscious feelings of resentment and anger. After the deal is done or the job is secured, these resentments sometimes erupt inappropriately later as gossiping, complaining, or an uncooperative streak.

Remember, if you make a deal, then you have to live with it. Low BEQ professionals are unable to negotiate for what they want, and then afterwards they blame others. This type also tends to snoop around to see what compensation or business arrangements other colleagues have negotiated for themselves, and then cry foul or unfair if it tops what they have managed to win for themselves. Some professionals know how to drive a hard but fair bargain that serves their best interests. Others do not, and this is an endless source of resentment, conflict, and office politics in the workplace, even as management tries to keep information about benefits and compensation strictly confidential.

The more disagreeable types who overreach, insisting they have their own way in everything, and win every deal point, also perform poorly in negotiations, by demanding too much and alienating others. It's not uncommon to see professionals compensate for a lack of self-confidence, by pushing to always have their ideas implemented, and becoming aggressive and uncooperative when they don't get their way. Unsurprisingly, not playing well with others, due to a relentless need to stand out, shine, and win, usually nixes their chances for promotion and a shot at leadership positions, even though their greatest desire may be to be appointed head honcho.

Three keys to effective negotiation:

- A successful negotiator is not personally invested in a perfect outcome. They are pragmatic in accepting compromise on agenda items, in order to move a deal forward to a satisfactory close, even if it pans out differently than initially hoped for or anticipated.
- An effective negotiator knows that the bottom line in any negotiation is getting what is absolutely necessary to make progress. This includes not overplaying a hand, and not caving due to pressure or for fear of losing out.

- A realistic negotiator understands and accepts there is always a risk that they may come up empty ended and be forced to move on to the next opportunity.

You win some, you lose some. But the higher your Business EQ, the higher your batting averages will be as a savvy negotiator.

Getting Comfortable With Flexibility

Very often we start a negotiation with single-minded focus on just one objective or outcome. Consequently, we refuse to compromise on terms we've convinced ourselves we *must* have. We lose when we forget that adjustments, which present no material adverse effect, should be considered, even if it looks like we've capitulated on an important point.

Those who can't remain flexible and entertain acceptable compromises, and who instead get emotional, upset or offended, and shut down talks, are guaranteed to lose in deal after deal. When you start feeling cornered and reactive in a negotiation, remember:

- Discipline yourself to step back and relax for a spell to refresh your perspective. If necessary, take a few days before objecting too vigorously to a proposition that appears unfavorable.
- Think about deal points creatively, seeing the challenge from all angles.
- Look for ways to modify a request so it works for you, even if it's not what you initially had in mind.
- Avoid getting hung up on a fear that the opposition is "beating" you or making you look inadequate.
- Stay focused on winning as much as possible—not everything, which may mean conceding certain key points.

Here's a classic example of an impasse often encountered in a contract negotiation: Each party to a contract typically wants any future contract dispute to be heard in courts within their home state. But sometimes the commercial law in an opponent's state might actually be preferable for settling a dispute. In any event, instead of arguing over which state law should govern the contract, it can be better to remain silent on this point, and let the facts of any future case determine what state law is applicable. This move is one that nervous, risk-averse lawyers have trouble with, so it creates a needless stalemate.

Read Your Opponent

When you first meet with an opponent, register, without over think-ing or assuming too much, your first impressions. Did he or she seem very polite or very rigid? How about aggressive? Or authoritative? Or over friendly? Typically, how a person first projects themselves is based on their underlying temperament and emotional drivers, beliefs, or hang-ups—or calculations. Consider what inner temperament may be undergirding the outer persona. For example, very rigid, aggres-sive types are often bullies, afraid of losing or appearing weak. And, accordingly, they may have trouble compromising, for fear of looking inadequate.

Remember that you don't know what you don't know, including how desperately your opponent may need what they are negotiating for. The less invested we are in an outcome, the more we can adopt a take-it-or-leave-it attitude. At times, however, securing a deal is so critical to one of the party's involved that they will seemingly overpay or relinquish important deal points to get what they must have.

In these situations, those on the other side of the negotiating table cannot believe their good luck in getting more than they thought pos-sible, but often fail to take full advantage of the situation. They may even walk away and regret "leaving money on the table," not sensing until later that they could have demanded and received even more than they did.

The lesson is not to project onto an opponent what you think a deal is worth to them. Stay alert and try to read their level of urgency and need, and take full advantage when you sense you can drive a very hard bargain. In most cases, there is no reason to feel guilty if you think your counter-part on the other side of the table overpays or gives away too much. What looks like a bad deal to you could represent a critical piece in their plan for business or career triumph.

Taking Risks

If you're afraid to lose, you will lose. Sometimes a negotiation is like a gamble in which you must be willing to lose something tangible, like a down payment, or a compromise on liquidated damages, if one party defaults on the contract. Remember:

- Never lose more than you can realistically afford, but understand that risk of loss is often part of the equation. High risk often brings high reward, as the saying goes.
- Recognize those times when compromise is not possible, and you need to move on, either cutting existing losses, or abandoning the deal altogether.
- Don't feel like you've failed if the terms of any negotiation cannot be resolved to your complete satisfaction. The strongest negotiating approach is to be open to possibly not getting what you want and having your negotiation appear unsuccessful, even having a deal or need fall though.
- Remember that too many compromises make for an unfavorable arrangement, which will hamper any chance of future success. So, to win, you have to risk walking away. And rely on the fact that there always another opportunity going forward.

Strategies for Getting Your Deal

Reasoning

Use logic that others may not immediately see to win in a negotiation, sometimes by pointing out how an opponent's specific request may in fact not serve them. A good example of this is when your adversary wants a contract to start based on an earlier date than when it is signed to include deals that have been done, say, earlier in a year. Point out that earlier deals are governed by old terms, which fail to include benefits and safeguards that are being presently negotiated. If your opponent is risk-averse, it's likely that, by pointing this fact out, you can get them to abandon "back dating" the terms of a new contract.

Manipulation

Cleary, we all manipulate in life, to a greater or lesser extent, consciously or unconsciously. For many, the term "manipulation" is repugnant and they feel uncomfortable if accused of it. If this describes you, be prepared to lose in any negotiation against an experienced negotiator. To the extent necessary, use whatever is possible to emotionally turn a transaction in your favor.

For example, as a way to win a point, characterize what the opposition is demanding as simply "unfair," and something that no other party you have ever negotiated with has asked for. People are too often socialized to believe that everything they do or ask for must sound reasonable and be "fair" to everyone. This is not how shrewd business negotiators think. So, don't fall victim to conventions or typical social "rules" or prescribed "good manners."

In a later chapter, we will discuss how street-smart operators often use both a relatively benign and also predatory form of emotional manipulation to negotiate or get what they want. They will feign anger, outrage, concern, or indifference to get ahead.

They are expert at taking an opponent's emotional temperature, or reading the room, seeing when irrational fears or emotions are at play, and manipulating them for advantage. The stakes can be high in business, and those who lack BEQ and street-smarts are too often at the mercy of savvy manipulators who play no-holds-barred.

Packing Up Your Briefcase and Walking Away

Winning sometimes demands you be prepared to walk away in any negotiation. Shutting down talks, and introducing distance, often leads the other side to reconsider their position. Any good negotiator knows that giving a deal ultimatum can be the ultimate trump card in winning. Don't be afraid to use it, but use it sparingly to maintain its effect.

The bottom line in any type of negotiation is to understand that the process typically involves risk taking. If you are afraid of taking measured risks, you cannot be a good negotiator. So, be honest with yourself, and be confident that there is always another opportunity if you do have to use the ultimate "take it or leave it" approach to get what you reasonably need.

CHAPTER 14

Working Skillfully With Workplace Emotions

Understanding Emotional Needs: A Key to Being Effective

Collaborating, partnering, or managing others requires understanding their emotional needs as well as your own. Otherwise, you won't get the most from them and, worse yet, you'll likely fail as a manager or colleague. And when emotional needs aren't met, or emotional limits are exceeded, business risk is created. By unintentionally humiliating someone in front of his or her peers, for example, you risk having your job, career, or business sabotaged, willfully or unintentionally, by that person.

When you manage people, you are, in effect, managing their emotional needs, which does not necessarily mean accommodating their emotional needs. The difference, of course, should be clear at this point—when needs are responsible and align with business objectives, they can be met. Otherwise they should be addressed with an honest and mature reality check and a discussion that sets proper expectations.

So how do you effectively work with a subordinate or associate's emotional needs?

- Start by understanding how working for someone else, or for a company, fits into a person's emotional makeup, value system, or zone of comfort.
- Some people's needs will be apparent. For those that are not, you'll need to be alert for clues that signal more difficult to discern drivers.
- Many needs are universal, while others are specific or idiosyncratic.

- Becoming more aware of your own personal wants and desires helps you to recognize similar needs in others.
- And, as we have already explored, paying attention to the people and associates that others seek out or attract can clue us into what makes them tick.

Emotional Needs and Employment

In thinking about it, we realize how so much more than mere financial gain drives most of us in business. Psychologists such as Abraham Maslow, who outlined his famous hierarchy of needs, give us a good framework for understanding the ascending levels of achievement that most humans aspire to and work toward:

- Satisfying survival needs that push us to put a roof over our heads and food in our stomachs.
- Establishing productive and emotionally rewarding relationships and community to undertake creative endeavors.
- Fully realizing our individual potential to be among those who achieve "peak experiences," which brings a profound sense of purpose, meaning, and satisfaction to life.

In pursuit of wide-ranging goals, we experience an array of complex, often healthy, and sometimes dysfunctional, emotional patterns, and drivers. People go to work and act out many and varied desires:

- The need for a "family" with membership in a collective, or even to secure parental-style support.
- A need for the workplace to be a place for sharing personal and professional problems and finding solutions.
- A place to get away from external problems or anxieties.
- Or alternatively, a place to create problems, drama and office politics, as a way to act out personal conflicts.

If you have but don't recognize such needs in yourself, you may react adversely when you encounter them in others and manage them poorly. So, let's kickstart your thinking about common emotional needs that might be satisfied in the work environment, how a number of them overlap, and how they might be true for you and the people you manage or encounter.

Financial Survival

We all need money. Some more than others. Those driven by financial greed often will not stop at shady or illegal business dealings to create as much wealth as possible, but most of us seek an honest day's work for an honest day's pay. Not always obvious, however, is the fact that emotional needs supersede or overtake financial needs more often than any of us realize.

People routinely satisfy ego or emotional needs at the expense of financial security. They will risk getting fired, blowing up a negotiation, deep-sixing a promotion, sabotaging a project, or perpetuating a lie, in order to scratch an emotional itch that they may or may not even understand.

A thin-skinned financial analyst may stick to his analysis and conclusions to avoid admitting he's made a careless or thoughtless mistake, unintentionally putting the business at risk. And those plagued by feelings of inadequacy or insecurity will be hostile and defensive, instead of open and responsive, when confronted with errors they have made or tried to cover up.

Most of us, when pressed, can find numerous instances of how we allowed emotions or fearful imaginings to hurt our career, our progress, a business project, or our wallet. How about you?

- Have you ever felt excluded from the inner workings of a business simply because, perhaps, you were not invited to a certain working lunch or meeting?
- Do you too easily read personal rejection or criticism into a boss or an associate's words?
- Do perceived slights or rejection make you feel like quitting, complaining, or fearful that you will not advance in your career?

Have you ever worked or known someone who has worked for a company that is on the financial edge? What feelings did this uncertainty engender in them or in you? Did it a create paralysis or a tailspin of worry? Did it prompt productive activity to find new opportunities, or a relaxed wait and see approach?

Stressful work situations flush out our default emotional settings and put on display underlying beliefs about ourselves, the world, and what we imagine is our place in it. For some, the loss of a job signals very real struggle or decline, while others transition easily into another situation, and still others are liberated to prosper more fully. Although not everything boils down to attitude and emotional makeup, strong Business Emotional Intelligence (BEQ) definitely guides us through stressful situations or transitions to a better outcome.

Job Security

For those who value loyalty and see work as an extension of family or as a support system, a job in corporate America can be disillusioning. "No one is indispensable" is a mantra that many of us learn the hard way. They key here is understanding the importance of fostering a commitment to our work, our continued development, and our performance, rather than just commitment to the company. This means performing our job to the best of our ability, so we have a track record that attracts prospects and continued opportunities.

Those with strong BEQ are under no illusion that they will be guaranteed a long-term position with a particular employer, no matter how well they perform. They know that it is by building a track record of excellent results for their resume that they ensure future employability.

Unfortunately, corporate America sometimes has little choice and often no hesitation about rolling over people in its search of profits or survival; an alarming reality for those who need an illusion of certainty about how tomorrow will be. Hanging on to a so-so job, because you mistakenly believe it offers security, may not ultimately be prudent.

Personal Identity

Many employees measure themselves by identifying with the company they work for. If the company has an excellent reputation, they feel they'll be thought of highly, while sometimes fearing they will be considered inferior if their place of business is failing. There is nothing wrong with wanting to work for a company whose reputation enhances our personal prestige as long as we acknowledge this as a motivating factor and don't take it too far.

It's not uncommon for the overly image conscious to make employment decisions based solely on corporate pedigree, believing that a company's high profile defines their personal value. They place this over securing more meaningful and relevant work opportunities or experience.

Working for a well-regarded company may well make aspirational types feel superior in social settings. They may also be preoccupied with status, in general, symbolized by luxury cars or possessions, an expensive wardrobe, costly travel and the "right" address, which could lead some to live beyond their means. The underlying desire is to use status, image, and reputation to impress others and feel successful, instead of hitting career milestones, which reflect personal accomplishments that feed genuine self-respect.

We're not suggesting that bolstering self-image by seeking tenure at a prestigious enterprise or institution is a problem in itself. Only when craving status is a driving need whose source goes unrecognized and undermines more important career considerations. The same goes for people you might hire. If the company's reputation suffers, because it falls on difficult times, status seekers may bail out rather than stick around to help right the ship.

Eliminating Irrational Anxieties

Using the workplace as a sanctuary or a personal support system, rather than as a stepping-stone to professional growth and progress, is not uncommon. Working for a company with trusted colleagues can provide a sense of inner peace and stability by eliminating irrational anxieties. Those who have difficulty handling problems, or making decisions, or encountering change, are less worried when they know there are colleagues to turn to for help in a familiar work setting.

The downside is that these dependent types often inadvertently miss opportunities in an effort to stay emotionally comfortable and secure. And this is precisely the point made earlier: The insecure make choices to stay in their emotional comfort zone and "settle" in their careers rather than explore their full potential.

Family Needs

Working for a company can seem akin to living at home with your parents—a nine-to-five version of family life. The job environment becomes, in effect, a substitute family:

- There's a head of the household, the boss, who's always there to tell you what to do.
- There are siblings—your coworkers—you can bond or squabble with when you need distractions.
- Decisions are easier because they're spread among coworkers and the boss, with everybody knowing their chores and responsibilities.
- And as a child looks to his parents for nurturing and survival, so do some employees look to bosses. When you're "good" or compliant, your parents pat you on the back and up your "spending" money. Your boss does the same, literally and figuratively.

And the analogies continue. There is nothing wrong with this scenario, as long as you keep matters in perspective and understand the dynamics at play. When operating as a manager, if you recognize and satisfy those working for you who have these needs, they will prosper—and so will you.

Along the same lines, many corporate employees dream about having their own business but never act on it for the very reason just discussed—they don't want to leave "home." They have a strong and often unconscious need to be in a family-like environment with parental authority guiding them. Not a problem, so long as it's honestly acknowledged as a factor in career decisions.

In fact, when people work for others, it's not unusual for them to have a severe attack of the "what ifs" when they think about venturing out, going into business for themselves, or moving on. What if this happens?

What if that happens? They talk themselves out of leaving, possibly missing a good opportunity in the process. The "what if" anxiety is often an excuse to avoid a move and courting discomfort. Going into their own business is like "leaving their family." And that's the real personal challenge that should be addressed—in effect, letting go of so-called security, real or imagined.

Acceptance

Most of us want to be accepted by others. It's how we were socialized in childhood—before we even knew how to fully evaluate why and to what extent acceptance was important, if at all. When we were accepted by our parents, and later our friends, we were happy, and sad when rejected, perhaps even upset.

It's often no different when working for a company. To be accepted, we have to please the boss—the parental figure. When we don't, we risk being fired or missing a promotion or a raise. So, to keep those working for you well-motivated, you must let them know they're accepted. And if doing this threatens or makes you uncomfortable, use it as a clue to an unprocessed attitude that could limit your management potential.

For acceptance seekers, being fired is the ultimate rejection, humiliating for some and devastating for others. They worry that their firing signals to the world that they are no good. Unfortunately, what others think is, to such worriers, often more important in determining personal worth than their recognition of their true value.

Never forget, when you place your personal value in the hands of others, you risk business suicide. Competitive, jealous, resentful, manipulative, and angry people are all around. They stand ready, consciously or otherwise, to undermine everyone else's confidence, through criticisms, snubs and other belittling actions. And they can smell your insecurity like blood in the water. So if your self-worth depends on what other people think, your career potential is in jeopardy.

Again, once you become aware of internal emotional drivers, such as the need for acceptance, recognize how it can trip you up. Seeing clearly your desire for acceptance is the beginning of uncovering how you may have adopted false premises on which you base your self-worth.

You must come to believe that you have value outside of the external and conditional approval you seek from others. Only then can you be assured that self-esteem will not be unfairly damaged by others. And so too, you, when working as a manager, must be attuned to, and carefully manage, similar needs in subordinates. Do it with maturity and kindness and they will likely respond with loyalty and dedication.

BEQ Case Study: You're Fired

Jenny tossed and turned and couldn't sleep. Tomorrow, she would tell Clark, her boss of six months, that she wanted to fire the PR firm he had recommended she hire, soon after the board had installed him as CEO. The PR firm just happened to be run by one of Clark's close personal friends. The firm was not effective and was using up a portion of Jenny's marketing budget that could be better spent elsewhere. She had explained to Clark how the company really were not ready for the expense of a retained PR firm yet, since their software product, undergoing upgrades, was months away from roll-out. Clark had argued and waved her off, until Jenny had relented and hired his friend's firm for a pretty penny three months earlier. Since then, the firm had been mostly on idle, as well as slow and sloppy in completing the couple of projects that Jenny had dreamed up for them to complete. Now members of Jenny's team were grousing that the PR firm was a waste of time and money that could be better used elsewhere.

Jenny rehearsed her talking points. She told Clark, over his objections, that she intended to put the PR firm on ice and end the retainer relationship until such time that it was really needed. She would then interview several agencies to ensure they hired a firm that was the best fit and not just convenient. Clark's annoyance was palpable as he glowered at her, while she gave her business reasoning. Jenny fired the agency that afternoon. And during the weeks that followed, she sensed that her relationship with Clark was going downhill. He was critical and irritable with her, sometimes dropping her from team meetings and calls.

Jenny was gripped with worry but tried not to panic by reading too much into Clark's behavior. That's why she was completely blindsided when he told her on their weekly one-on-one meeting, six weeks after she had fired the PR firm, that he was letting her go. She had performed well for two years in her role, he said, but he wanted someone on his team who felt like a better fit.

After being fired, Jenny left with a massive dent in her confidence and with a pile of recriminations. She went back on forth, telling herself that she should never have terminated the agency and provoked Clark's anger. But then she reminded herself that she had been acting in the company's best interests in putting an end to Clark's cronyism and self-dealing. Within six weeks, Jenny had a new role, and within six months, she had put the whole unfortunate episode into perspective.

Even though she had felt embarrassed and worried about what others were thinking when Clark fired her, Jenny realized that she had done the right thing. Her self-doubt faded, and she felt more confident for taking a principled stand and refusing to be intimidated. Soon former colleagues from her old firm were calling her. Clark, they said, was a self-dealing control freak. Some were afraid to speak up and risk being fired, too, but others were choosing to move on, knowing that, long term, they could never flourish in the type of environment that Clark had created.

CHAPTER 15

Spotting Saboteurs

Don't Overlook or Misread Problem People

How often do you miss obvious clues that a coworker or subordinate is undermining you for reasons we have already laid out? It's not uncommon for businesspeople to pursue emotional gratification to such an extent that business objectives and progress, fairness, and doing the right thing, become irrelevant. So, when a coworker or associate you've worked with for a long time surprises you with counterproductive conduct, this is your clue that you may be unconsciously filtering out sabotage—theirs and yours.

Let's look at behavioral traits that often signal destructive types. Again, not all-inclusive, this list outlines relatable categories to get you thinking about associates and their habits in a fresh way.

Failure-Prone Employees

The failure-prone drive us to distraction with unacceptable behavior, seeming to pursue disaster with relish: Late for work. Late for meetings. Missed deadlines. Massive typos in important communication. Intemperate acts and similar nonsensical conduct.

Failure-prone employees create one problem after another. Without professional help, they rarely change. Bosses who keep them around often do so to satisfy their own misguided needs. And, in these cases, it's likely that both are codependent personalities, subtlety, desperately, and unknowingly engaged in an emotionally complex relationship that is dragging each of them down. Such relationships often mirror crippled marriages, or partners who are engaged in smothering and self-limiting acts to distract each other from deeper inner issues that are too painful to openly address.

If you work with personalities who always create problems, and you've allowed the situation to continue without wondering why, entertain the possibility that you may have a need for someone who distracts you or makes you feel better about yourself, perhaps by serving up work product and conduct that are clearly inferior to your own. And maybe that's your clue to shed light on a bad habit you need to correct.

Failure-prone employees sometimes portray themselves as victims. They deceptively manipulate, sometimes as a child manipulates a parent, by making you feel sorry for them. If you end up doing their work, you may feel like the White Knight when you finish. You saved the day for them. And you feel good about it! But if you fall into this trap, you are complicit in their poor behavior.

If you're working with a subordinate whose performance you constantly complain about, consider that they might be failure-prone. And if you've held onto the relationship, you might be as well. The clues are in front of you: Do these colleagues always make the same mistakes that you inevitably catch and perhaps gossip or complain to others about? If so, be honest about your role or motivation in keeping this person around.

Firing them may not be the complete answer, particularly if you haven't resolved yet why you allowed the relationship to continue. If you do fire a failure-prone employee, your challenge will be to make sure you don't hire a replacement with similar problems, an inclination you may not recognize.

A Strategy for Handling the Failure-Prone

If you're entangled with a failure-prone employee or colleague:

- Explore any thoughts you have.
- Develop possible strategies to deal with them.
- Experiment with what you learn, seeing what works, if anything, and what doesn't.
- Consider changing their responsibilities or hiring an executive coach to help you work through the problem.
- Have an honest and open discussion with them, while understanding that discussion alone may not be enough. Problems

with strong emotional underpinnings often cannot be resolved by surface discussion.

- Force yourself to stop complaining. Once your mind clears, the chances are good that a solution will surface.
- Don't just chronically complain and allow the problem to run on without a resolution. Act on the matter and solve it.
- Ultimately, you may have to get out of the relationship.

Managing Negative Employees or Naysayers

As we've repeated, negativity is the single biggest career and business killer. Here we discuss it in the context of negative employees. We already explained how, for nervous managers, naysaying advisors or workers provide a safe rationale for not making go-forward decisions and a way to avoid taking any responsibility for their own negativity.

Negative employees and naysayers come in all shapes and sizes:

- They take the wind out of your sails when you're trying to solve business problems or innovate for progress, or when you express your hopes and dreams.
- They invariably have an answer for everything, and it's typically just two words: "too risky" or "won't work."
- They put a dampener on virtually every new discussion and idea—unless, of course, it's theirs.
- Racked with anxieties, they have a need to control everything, so they can stay in their unhappy, "happy" place.
- They often hide negative attitude behind oblique statements such as, "Oh, I hope it works out for you," in response to new directions or efforts you're pursuing.
- Most of what they say and do points maniacally to avoiding risk or to sabotage.
- They unrealistically feel any decision should be taken only if the outcome is certain, ignoring the reality that progress cannot be made without venturing into the unknown and risking outcomes.

- Surprisingly, they're often intelligent, using their keen analytical ability to convince you that they know how to move
  forward without risk. Don't fall for their risk-avoidance logic,
  unless you want to remain as limited or stuck as they are.

What's behind the negative attitude? While there is no one answer, more often than not, it is, once again, fear: Fear of change. Fear of looking stupid. Fear of being fired. Fear of the unknown. Fear of moving out of the comfort zone. Fear of loss of control. Fear of life itself!

Negative people are often jealous of those who get ahead, never acknowledging that their own mindset is the main reason they're behind. And jealously often drives them to make sure others don't overtake them or even flat-out fail. The unfortunate part is that negative people are often talented and could be productive if they were not crippled. For them, it's more important to feel better by holding others back than by moving forward themselves.

A Strategy for Handling "Negaholics"

There's no single solution for handling a negative employee or associate. They can be very competitive, blocking your progress at every turn—sometimes quite creatively. If you see that someone's out-and-out risk avoidance, which they couch as prudent business rationale, starts to slow you down, you may have to limit their input or risk failure. And when you do, expect them to act out or manipulate, by pouting or going totally silent on you in meetings. In any event, if you can't control their negative influence, they must be countered, by making sure they don't dominate conversations or control situations.

Let's say you're in a key business discussion and a negative employee is throwing cold water on everyone's suggestions, confronting them directly is risky, possibly inviting an avalanche of defensiveness, cover-ups, and even a personal attack. You stand a better chance of managing their negativity indirectly, with such statements as, "Let's see what the market tells us about our strategy, instead of telling ourselves 'no', and talking ourselves out of a viable idea, right out of the gate." But, even then, be prepared.

Remember that negative people are manipulative, so expect them to be visibly but subtlety uncooperative. And be careful, they are prone to working covertly behind the scenes, sabotaging you at every turn. Ultimately, you may have no choice but to exclude them completely from the decision-making process.

Employees Who Never Disagree

Employees who never tell you what they really think, or when they disagree, are likely to be unconsciously self-destructive and can inadvertently impede you. This is the proverbial "Yes Man." Failing to recognize a "Yes Man," or needing one around, is another clue to your unexamined and unproductive beliefs.

What's behind their yes-to-everything approach? Don't mistake it for genuine agreement, when it more likely flags a reluctance to express an honest opinion, for fear, founded or unfounded, that you, the boss, or their peers, will get angry, reject, punish, or expose them to criticism for their "dumb" opinions or statements. With certain bosses, this fear may be entirely justified. But what the "Yes Man" never realizes is that such blind compliance does not serve him or anyone else.

A Strategy for Handling Yes Men

The key to working with "Yes Men" is reassuring them that expressing an honest opinion, even when it disagrees with yours, is perfectly acceptable and, in fact, welcome. But you must be consistent and follow through, by creating an environment that demonstrates how contrary opinions and active consensus building are welcomed as productive.

Quiet Employees

Employees who never or rarely express an opinion, or offer input, can create serious challenges. Although often talented, these typically anxious, shy, or sometimes low self-worth individuals prefer to avoid mentioning problems that should be addressed.

They suffer in silence, are sometimes depressed, and are clearly less productive. If they're having trouble with a customer, for example, they may not tell you, resulting in the loss of an account that could have been saved if addressed in a timely manner. So, don't be lulled by a worker who says little, thinking they have everything under control, or have no issues with you, their job, or the business.

A Strategy for Handling Quiet Types

As with employees that never disagree, you, as a manager, need to help these reluctant talkers get comfortable enough to speak openly with you, particularly when they encounter problems. Pointing out their reticence directly may work, but it's usually better to slowly engage them in small talk until they feel at ease in opening up.

This is usually best done one-on-one, rather than is a group setting, until they are ready to be more talkative in a group. Be consistently supportive. Understand that the process of getting them comfortable can take a long time, but is often worth the investment since they will likely appreciate your support and eventually blossom.

Hot-Tempered Employees

Those who easily lose their temper are clearly problem employees. Invariably, they have personal problems too complex to address here and which may need professional guidance in anger management. Ultimately, a hot-tempered employee shuts down open communication.

Typically, hot heads don't relate well to others, and, as you would suspect, often have poor interpersonal skills. Their temper can be the way they keep people at a distance or otherwise manage painful feelings that surface when interacting with people. As with any other problem employee, your tolerating this behavior is a clue to an underlying stumbling block.

A Strategy for Handling Hot Heads

Short of having a hot-tempered employee seek professional help, there's little you can do, other than fire them, to ensure they don't disrupt the team or the business. If their problem is deep-rooted, talking to them directly about the temper issue rarely solves the problem. A bad temper is simply something most people have little control over, unless they actively commit to effective self-help strategies.

Passive-Aggressive Employees

Passive-aggressive employees demand that you be on your toes to detect when they might be silently sabotaging you. They come in a variety of personality wrappers: some appear as negative, some as glad-handers. Their passive-aggressive nature may show up as sullenness, procrastination, resistance, withdrawal from participation in the business process, resentment, stubbornness, or deliberate and repeated failure to follow through on work projects.

In any event, they're clearly self-destructive and can easily create morale problems, in addition to being very difficult to manage. The *first* time someone acts or gossips destructively behind your back, this is your clue that you may be dealing with a passive-aggressive personality.

A Strategy for Handling the Passive Aggressive

For hard-core passive-aggressive types, the best solution is getting them professional help, whether it's an executive coach or a therapist. That may not be possible, and firing them, particularly those likely to take advantage of the employment laws, is challenging. So carefully document events that surround their lack of performance or participation.

These folks do what they want, knowing that if you push them out, they can use whatever rules are available in law to collect damages. They, unfortunately, do a disservice to employees who are legitimately discriminated against or otherwise treated unfairly in the workplace.

Are All Emotionally Destructive Individuals Bad for Business?

A discussion of self-destructive employees wouldn't be complete without asking whether, in the often cut-throat business world, some might offer value in certain situations. And, interestingly, they do. But you must manage them carefully.

For example, an aggressive Napoleonic personality can achieve quick and positive results when given absolute control as long as his or her behavior is in sync with the business needs. They are often promoted or brought in when a business is in crisis to do whatever is necessary to turn it around. Firing people is a breeze for them. Manipulating creditors is pure joy. This is playtime! These personalities go into overdrive when given free rein to do anything that gets results. And they take full advantage of their mandate, regardless of the social cost to the community or to the existing employees.

But they often become destructive to the organization once the business crisis is resolved. Everyone inside becomes a target when the challenge is over. They start attacking others to avoid looking at themselves. Superiors are suddenly stupid and working for them becomes aggravating. They often let everyone in the company know their feelings. And, when that happens, it's time to kick them out.

In conclusion, there are many different types of employees who create work or morale problems that torpedo business progress for everyone involved. If you, as a manager, find you have indulged a problem employee for years, this demands that you look at your own motivations and be honest about why you've put up with this situation, and what perverse benefit you're getting out of the status quo. Clearly, as a last resort, when talking to them or getting them professional help doesn't work, problem employees should be let go.

CHAPTER 16

When Saboteurs
Are In Charge

Problem Managers Destroy Careers

Why, considering the countless business books and courses that offer solid strategy after strategy on managing people, are there so many poor managers? Particularly when all that's needed is to offer obvious incentives: challenging work, positive feedback, financial security, and a feeling of acceptance and accomplishment?

Low Business EQ is often the root of the problem, which can include unconscious acting out that sinks all chances of success and pollutes the work environment. As well as pushing agendas that have nothing to do with getting the most out employees, but instead are geared to serving the manager's ego and emotional needs, no matter how counter-productive.

Being stuck with a problem manager can spell career disaster. So it's critical for your business well-being that you gain a clear perspective and assessment of your manager and, if you can't change the relationship dynamics, find a way out.

Classic Destructive Managers

Destructive managers are walking time bombs, who often possess control and manipulation techniques that they have finely honed over many years. People of low ethical standards attempt to boost themselves by forcing others to their emotional knees, or by making sure no one working for them threatens their well-being or status, real or imagined. Eventually, they cripple their own career, along with the careers of subordinates, as well as the business interests they're involved with.

How do you spot a destructive manager? Sometimes it's difficult. The easy-to-spot are egotistical, rarely listening, and disrespectful to everyone. By treating others with disrespect, they have, at least in their mind, put themselves in a superior role. The irony is that, as boss, they're already in the one-up position. But that's not enough. They must assert, at every turn, that they are smarter and more worthwhile than anyone else.

Others are harder to detect. They're the slick personalities who look good on the surface, but who are so entrapped by their emotional conflicts that their decisions undermine the interests of all involved in their business sphere. So, if your gut tells you something might be amiss with a boss, or just not adding up from a business perspective, patiently look for clues that point to covert motivations. And be particularly alert to insights you might gain from office gossip about the boss's demeanor or tactics.

A destructive manager's style makes him feel powerful or compensates for what she lacks personally. Crushing others may be her way of showing her importance to a world she fears thinks little of her. After all, who but an important person could take such liberties with others? Gender is irrelevant. Both men and women indulge.

On a short-term basis, these managers may produce results. A company in trouble can be pulled together by a hard-nosed, brutal management style. Over the long term, that's another matter. Destructive executives often take down the business and, at least for the moment, the emotional and business lives of the people under them, along with themselves.

Many destructive managers are angry or frightened, riddled with conflicts about who they are, and unsure of their capabilities. Some are chronically dissatisfied with themselves. Others are running from feelings they don't want to address, most of which have likely been irrationally carried over from childhood, or from bad business or career experiences.

Unfortunately, no matter how well they do, nothing eliminates the destructive feelings that drive their attitude and behavior. But they frantically try—by bullying, belittling or manipulating. Invariably, they self-destruct with actions so obviously dumb or outlandish that their career is brought to a surprising halt. Perhaps because they make a series of bad business decisions, or create unnecessary risks in the workplace, inviting retribution and hostile workplace or discrimination lawsuits.

Destructive Management—A Double-Edged Sword

A bad management style hurts you, whether you're the culprit who's deploying it, or a victim struggling under it. In either case, a willingness to prolong suffering under emotionally destructive leadership is a bad sign. So, if you're a manager, the next time you are rude or insensitive to someone working for you, identify every thought going through your mind—such as an argument at home, or a criticism from your boss, or an ancient insecurity. Even if you think there is no connection, you will undoubtedly find, by paying attention to these incidents, and your thoughts over time, a recurring pattern that is hampering your progress.

And, if you're the victim of a destructive manager, do the same: pay attention to your feelings and thoughts, whenever you're treated poorly, to see how you may be complicit in keeping yourself in a dysfunctional environment.

The Destructive Manager Trap

A destructive manager can psychologically trap you, particularly if you've arrived on the business scene with certain basic misconceptions. For example, if you've been led to believe that a rude and aggressive go-getter exemplifies what a successful manager is all about, you may not see that you're being mistreated, and think the persistent hazing is good for you and par for the business course. This will eventually erode your confidence and stymie your career.

Bad bosses like to assert that your faults and shortcomings are the sole reason you are unable to make progress, browbeating you into the belief that little you do is right, and reducing you to a state of perpetual defensiveness. If you buy into their claims, you're finished. Of course you have limitations, but these are not the people to coach you out of them. Clearly, their personal style is hard for most people to cope with.

So, if you're a perfectionist or very self-critical, be alert to being emotionally trapped by a put-down management style. Chances are good that you won't see when you're being unfairly criticized, especially if it mirrors your own self-criticism. You'll likely be consumed with eliminating all possible criticism, rather than working in your best interest, never realizing that putting an end to criticism from an emotionally conflicted manager is impossible. The bottom line: A desire to do a perfect job, coupled with being too self-critical, can sink you, because it prevents you from maintaining a balanced perspective and realistic view of yourself.

Protecting Yourself From Destructive Management

The best protection against destructive managers is to avoid working for them, but that's not always possible, since they exist at virtually every level of management across the business sphere. The real danger, as we said, is being blind to their harmful tendencies when you encounter them. Spending years dealing with a wrecking ball of a boss can waste valuable career time that you can never reclaim.

Spotting destructive management techniques requires effort. If you indulge in constantly undermining yourself, chances are you'll never realize the extent to which critical managers unfairly and irrationally hold you back. If it's chronic, you may need someone you trust to give you a perspective on what is happening. If you don't, you'll risk putting your career on hold while you fruitlessly chase approval from managers who will never give it to you.

A Strategy—A Chance for Personal Development

Confronting a destructive manager is risky. Chances are you won't be successful in convincing them that they are being unfair, and you may force them underground. If there's no immediate way out for you, the best you can hope for is to cope with the abuse. Instead of complaining, take a short- and a long-term approach to the problem. But keep one thing firmly in mind: you will never change a destructive manager's approach and behavior toward you. Acknowledging this difficult truth is absolutely necessary in order for you to deal with the situation realistically.

Your short-term solution is to move yourself off the firing range, by accepting that you're not the cause of the poor treatment. Remind yourself of this at every opportunity. Make a sign with "I am not the cause" on it, and paste it on your bathroom mirror. Look at it every morning. This may provide some relief in managing your feelings while following through on a long-term solution, which must be to find a new job.

Since you may be stuck in the situation for a while, make the best of it by developing your emotional awareness. Try to gain insight into yourself, by watching how you react emotionally. If your boss stomps on you or makes you angry, explore if this is because the criticism inflames what you already fear is true about yourself. Most of us get hurt or angry when a punch lands on a sore spot. It's easy to become reactive if our performance is criticized, when we already feel insecure in our job and abilities.

Alternatively, if we feel self-confident, we might take even harsh feedback as constructive, provided it is well-founded. The key in developing your awareness is to honestly explore why another's comments or behavior disrupt you. Working for an abusive boss is a great way to review and reorganize your emotional side, so you learn to treat yourself fairly and maintain your emotional equilibrium when under attack.

Finally, in developing your long- and short-term strategies, use your Development Diary to track your thoughts and feelings. Identify thoughts and self-talk that that tell you deserve to be treated poorly. All of this will help you frame the problem so you can gather your resources to put yourself back on track.

Positive Management May Be a Personal Challenge

A discussion of destructive managers would not be complete without pointing out a plausible reason that a positive management style may fall by the wayside. The golden rule suggests that we treat others as we would want to be treated. It's possible that, for certain managers and subordinates, being treated poorly works well with their psychology. Being emotionally mistreated, rather than treated with respect, may feel more comfortable, or at least more familiar, to them, for a variety of complicated reasons. And each may project this preference for ill treatment onto those who are either overseeing them, or working for them. In addition, people with poor self-regard often and unknowingly find it more comfortable to be in an unsupportive environment that distracts from their inner struggle.

There are other reasons some managers eschew a supportive management style. They may have a belief about how a successful manager behaves based on early training or influential role models. Never stopping to ask if the shoddy management style they unthinkingly adopt is worthy and serves them, their career, or business.

To make matters even more challenging, it's entirely possible that constructive or supportive managers may look weak to the unsophisticated. And managers who are unsure of themselves certainly want to avoid looking weak. If you're finding any of this hard to believe, stop and think about who and what society often glamorizes—the ruthless go-getter; the robber baron or hard-charging captain of industry; the cold calculating operator, who must get results regardless of human costs.

Add to this the unfortunate fact that many businesspeople believe that talking tough and bulldozing subordinates burnishes their reputation with others, and it's easy to see how poor management techniques take hold. It often requires guts to manage in a positive and affirming manner. And that can happen only when people are secure within themselves— well balanced and with high BEQ.

If you are working for a destructive manager, make no mistake, your career and talents will be jeopardized. Stay alert and step back from any self-critical aspect of yourself to view the situation more objectively. If you're destructively managing others, be assured that this will inevitably cost you. In either situation, you need to take a hard look at what is occurring and seek short- and long-term solutions to a destructive management style—especially your own.

CHAPTER 17

Pulling Together What You've Learned

Examine and Reexamine What's Motivating You

Building BEQ requires routinely and honestly evaluating your progress against stated business or career goals. Periodically reexamine what you tell the world and yourself you want in business, whether it's a top management position; a good career track; a worthwhile, fulfilling, and interesting job; financial security or wealth; social impact, or something else.

Take responsibility for any lack of progress. What we proclaim we want from our career and business life often does not jibe with what our underlying emotional wants and agenda dictate. When there's a disconnect between our conscious goals and what we need unconsciously to remain emotionally comfortable, we flounder, stall, or even fail.

Make Sure Your Real Business Goal Is Success

Notice how a pattern of emotional storms and negative dynamics often play out across business organizations, teams, and partnerships of all kinds? How many times have you seen emotional or anxious professionals act out inappropriately in a work setting to relieve internal discomfort, at the expense of their best business interests? The same emotional self-sabotage that you see in others may also plague you and is on show to all. Even when you cannot see it, others can.

Angry outbursts and temper tantrums, used as emotional venting or coping mechanisms, are an obvious violation of business etiquette, while more subtle behaviors are harder to spot but also pernicious. Within business partnerships in particular, a pattern of subtle aggression and needling can evolve that poisons the groundwork of both the relationship and the business. Left to go on for too long, uncontrollable and unproductive feelings between partners, and the reactions they trigger, can cripple or destroy even the most profitable and flourishing enterprise.

A partner's rude behavior brings an end to a viable business, when the other partners or associates can no longer tolerate it. When feelings take over, it's often no longer possible, without intervention, to systematically and rationally address and solve business relationship challenges, and keep business decision making and cooperation on track. Emotional needs come first and business viability drops by the wayside—to everyone's detriment. By contrast, by keeping feelings under control, an offended or perturbed partner has a solid chance of resolving conflicts to his personal benefit.

Avoid Projection and Mind Reading

Projection is a psychological concept that is easy to understand intellectually, but sometimes difficult to grasp emotionally. Projection, explained simply, means we project thoughts and feelings onto others that belong to us alone, and which exist in our mind and not in the minds of others. It's as if we are telling ourselves a story that we have constructed, and then we act as though others share our private narrative.

Why we project inner thoughts or feelings is complex and beyond the scope of this book, but good BEQ ensures we don't fall into the trap of believing that others share our irrational thoughts about a given situation or about ourselves, especially at those times when we are feeling anxious, worried, fearful, or lacking in confidence.

When we tell ourselves that we are not worthy of a promotion, of winning a new account, or of securing funds from an investor, we run the risk of projecting these beliefs onto the exact parties we need to impress with our talents. We unknowingly infect them with our stinking thinking in subtle ways, by how we talk and act, until we undermine any confidence they may have in us, just as we have undermined our own self confidence.

One form of projection manifests as "impostor syndrome," when a professional, no matter how talented, successful, and deserving, is convinced that they are merely fooling others into believing that they are competent and worthwhile. Underlying feelings of inadequacy poison the well. Instead of projecting confidence and a relaxed can-do spirit, those with impostor syndrome live in fear that supporters and backers will eventually see through them, until this fear becomes a self-fulfilling prophecy, which eventually erodes the esteem and support others offer them.

If you are watching a personal movie in which you feature as more of a zero than a hero, it's critical that you rein in irrational self-doubt. We all feel uneasy when facing new situations or growth opportunities, but past achievements should remind us that we have what it takes to master a new process or challenge. Those with strong BEQ know how to put fear and self-doubt into perspective and manage feelings that threaten to sink them as they tackle unchartered waters. "Act as if" and "Never let them see you sweat" are two mantras that are well used by those with BEQ.

The decision makers we encounter on the path to progress, be it a loan officer at a bank, a new sales prospect, or a hiring manager, cannot read our minds. They are not watching our personal movie, in which we are racked with fear of failure and self-doubt. If we project confidence, they are likely to see competence and not incompetence.

In fact, very often, business associates have a vested interest in assuming the best about us and believing that we are the right person for the job at hand. It makes their lives easier to think that we are the solution to the problem they face. No need for them to work any harder, or look any further, if they believe that we are the answer and sitting right in front of them. The goal is not to undermine their positive assumptions:

- Don't over talk in a situation where you are nervous or unsure.
- Don't bring in irrelevant details, questions, or doubts.
- Keep conversations brief, upbeat, and to the point. For example, "I am looking forward to this new position and working hard to make the business even more successful." Or "This loan or investment will ensure we build the business and take it to the next level."
- Statements should be forward looking, optimistic, and brimming with optimism and confidence that reassures others.

Those we encounter in business are usually weighed down with their own fear of failure. They don't need the extra burden of ours.

Another way we project is that we may judge or evaluate others as we evaluate ourselves:

- If we secretly lack confidence, we may not believe another's claims or belief in their future efforts or success, even if their track record demonstrates that they know how to win.
- If we are not hard-working or diligent, it is all too easy to suspect others of being lazy or ineffective.
- And conversely, if we are honest, we may assume or project honesty onto untrustworthy associates, who count on this to get away with dishonest dealing.

When we look out into the world, we are looking into a mirror and not through a window is one way of expressing the idea of projection. The key to working effectively with people, therefore, is to always be aware of the possibility that you could be projecting any of your good or bad feelings and notions onto them or the situation. It takes practice to remove personal filters, biases, expectations, and assumptions, in order to pay close attention to a new person who comes into your business orbit:

- Stay focused and observant.
- Capture your observations and impressions by taking notes.
- Try to be as objective as possible.
- Sort through your impressions later to construct an accurate picture of who or what a particular person or situation is.

We are herd creatures that want to huddle with like-minded others, but we must first validate that those we conduct business with are credible and trustworthy before we get too close. This takes time. And projecting inaccurately onto a business associate is a major stumbling block. We can never really penetrate another's persona, but it's important that we work to assemble as accurate a picture of reality as possible when assessing business players or work mates.

Take Control of Your Future: Acknowledge Business Reality and Trust Your Gut

One more important point: Going forward, use your gut instincts to help guide the way. If you suspect a decision is based on emotion and not on sound logic, trust your gut and look more closely to test that the decision makes business sense. The suspicion in your gut is your first clue that something could be amiss. Don't second guess yourself simply because you're initially relying on your instincts. Trust them. But understand that your gut feelings are not always reliable. Think of them more as an early-warning system, alerting you to dig deeper to confirm or allay concerns and piece together a more accurate picture.

Common Emotional Issues That Drive Bad Decisions

Business decisions that satisfy feelings and not legitimate demands are bad for you and the business you're in. In corporate America, for example, many well-meaning decision makers often act to protect their job security and their salary and bonus first, and the profitability and future success of the company is a far distant second.

Here are common types of emotional undercurrents that can lead you or people you're working with, or for, down the wrong path.

Anxiety-Driven Decisions

Anxiety is ubiquitous and contaminating. It requires an effective strategy to prevent it from influencing how we make decisions.

- Step one is bringing anxiety to the surface where we can recognize and manage it.
- Write your anxieties down.
- Talk them over with a friend.
- Make sure that you keep them in check, so they don't nudge you into taking action you will regret, until you can get a handle on the problem.

- If anxiety continues to control you, consider getting professional coaching or mentoring to develop effective strategies for short circuiting its effects.

Be aware, though, that healthy anxiety is a fact of business life and a motivating force. There is no way to eliminate it, only to manage or cope with it. Any overreaching need to be anxiety-free in business is unrealistic. Bumps in the business road inevitably create stress. So, when anxiety surfaces, your challenge is to make sure that you don't inadvertently sabotage progress by simply wanting to stamp it out.

Whenever you feel the urge to emotionally act out, dig deep, and put power back into your business life, by being honest about what you're really trying to achieve and reject emotional impulses. By keeping a clear business perspective, you're less likely to make decisions that keep you emotionally comfortable, but don't move you forward. And if you catch others acting out of irrational anxiety, gently point it out and offer reassurance. If you do this skillfully, there is a good chance you'll help them settle and think and act with greater clarity, which they will likely appreciate.

Some employees prefer an established or mature business environment where there is an almost boring routine and no nail-biting events. Others thrive in startups or fast-growing ventures that bring a barrage of daily challenges and new problems to solve. These latter types may describe themselves as adrenaline junkies, who thrive on chaos and stress.

It's easy to see then that finding employees who are temperamentally suited to a business's specific stage in its lifecycle and culture is important. Anxiety might kickstart some employees but shut others down. As businesses evolve and develop, they often see a shift in the employees they attract. As an operation becomes more stable, it's not unusual to see the thrill seekers jump ship in search of a new fast ride. Matching staff to corporate culture as it evolves is a delicate balance.

Frustration-Based Decisions

Even the most talented among us may have a tendency to give up when frustration sets in, when the going gets tough, or when hoped-for outcomes take too long appear. It's understandable. When everything comes to a tumbling halt, when plans go astray, or when the pursuit of the goal seems endless, all sorts of bad feelings surface, including pessimism, hopelessness, depression, even panic.

If running into speed bumps on your business path makes you doubt what you're doing, question if it's worth all the effort, and fear it will never work out, instead of abandoning the project, look deeper into your psyche. Realize that quitting is often just a way to put a stop to frustration, uncertainty about future outcomes, or fear of failing.

Winners with high BEQ develop techniques for putting such negative emotions into perspective, by taking a break, talking with mentors or cheerleaders, reframing the challenge, or simply pushing through what they feel is a brick wall. Those who are unknowingly self-defeating might just isolate in their worry. They refuse to rationally think through and understand that setbacks and frustration are often not long lasting and eventually pass. If they really want to suicide their mission, self-saboteurs will speak to negative friends and family, who are only too ready to reassure them that they are right to give up.

Those who have played competitive sports early on in life have an advantage in managing such dilemmas. They are familiar with the pain and frustration of training, drilling, competing, failing, and losing. They have techniques for keeping their head in the game and the determination to stay the course and cross the finishing line, even if where they end up is not where they had originally intended.

Enterprising spirits dream of having their own business. Since it's true that 80 percent of small businesses fail, perseverance is a key quality for would-be entrepreneurs. Those who succeed are often not the ones with the most talent or best idea, but rather the ones that are conscientious and persistent. They keep on keeping on, managing their fears and worries, celebrating small successes, learning from mistakes and remaining optimistic, until eventually they get a toe hold on success and keep building. They know that success comes to success and are willing to ride out failure, until they are in the winner's enclosure, no matter how modest their initial triumph.

Is the Project Your Baby?

Falling in love with an ill-conceived project or idea will go nowhere fast. The so-called passion projects often motivate us, but it's not unusual for people to cling to a dream that is not viable. And if they lack the flexibility to mold their concept into a business that has a chance of working, then curtains will inevitably close on the idea. Adapting and rerouting, going where the market dictates, is essential for any startup to avoid winding up on the failure heap.

Passion is a must-have quality for entrepreneurs, along with a willingness to stick with an idea for years before turning a profit. But passion and tenaciousness are usually coupled with a profound understanding and real-world validation that their business will pay off once they get if off the ground.

If a concept or project becomes nothing more than your way of saying, "Look at how creative I am" and you can't see that self-image or stubbornness are really driving you, you may miss where true opportunity lies. There is a whole class of wannabe entrepreneurs who fancy themselves as creative or big-idea people, always dreaming up and pitching hot new business concepts that never get traction, because their goal is to keeping circling the field and never really get in the game. Alternatively, other professionals become consumed with building an outstanding pedigree by amassing scholarly credentials, which they never translate into concrete business activity. They are passionate about learning and not doing.

Our Way of Experiencing Others May Create Blocks

Starting a business or new career path can be a tenuous affair. We put down tender roots that can be easily destroyed before they take hold. To give a fragile new endeavor a fighting chance, we have to shield if from negative, misguided, or poorly informed advisors that we may invite into our trust circle.

Always entertaining the *possibility* that an advisor's or associate's business counsel or instruction may be tainted by unconscious and destructive emotions, illusions, or inappropriate beliefs, will keep your own thinking clearer.

Realize that, while there are always good guiding principles to steer a business, there is no hard-and-fast rule book. It's just you and your ingenuity and BEQ. "How it's done" is whatever you need to do to stay in the arena, as you build a career or a business enterprise. It's no easy task to break so-called rules and change the way you have been taught to think about how business works. But being sovereign, autonomous, thinking and acting for yourself, are high-BEQ traits that pay dividends.

Many years ago, salespeople, who were trained to make cold telephone calls to develop business or generate customer demand, were paid a dollar for every "no" they received. This small payment helped diminish feelings of failure or rejection. A "no" was clearly not worth as much as a "yes," but it was worth a dollar.

A well-trained salesperson can confront nonstop rejection without becoming discouraged. They understand the math that tells them only a tiny number of prospects will ultimately buy from them, but that tiny number is often enough to ensure they earn a good living. They are focused on results, on plowing through all of the noes to get to a yes. So they are not caught up in rejection that's simply a by-product of the numbers game that is selling.

BEQ Case Study: Endless Effort to Win Investment Dollars

When Louis tried to raise money to start his first business—software and accounting support for small businesses, he thought that contacting around 50 potential investors would net him a backer. By the time he finally found someone to invest in his startup, Louis had toiled for over 18 months and contacted hundreds of people, including anyone that could help connect him to a funding source. Louis admitted to becoming discouraged at times, but his previous stint in software sales had primed him for the long haul and the extensive networking and selling that it took to secure investment dollars. Louis understood that he could persevere where others might give up. After all, if starting a business were easy, he figured, everyone would do it.

Stop Trying to Be Right

A need to be right can distort your ability to make good business decisions. And once a decision is made, the same need can block or distort seeing how rerouting may be necessary as the process plays out. Adding fuel to the fire, your pesky need to be right can completely eliminate any chance of success.

Those with high BEQ focus not on being right, but on finding success, in whatever form it takes. Trying to figure out the perfect course of action is nothing more than creating an illusion to allay fear. You can't predict what will happen. Success is something quite different than being right. Success reflects the humility to go wherever the main chance takes you and not where you are determined to go to prove your thesis.

Unfortunately, business schools and corporate America make a meal out of believing that the "right" course can be set before you start. And if you've bought into that belief, you've been misled. Accomplished business performers understand that success is often intuitive: a trial and error rerouting process layered over with common sense, clear thinking, and hard-won experience. So get into action and always be open to redirecting your focus and efforts, until you get results that benefit you, and not necessarily the results you anticipated.

Don't be the person with an answer in search of a problem. Be the person who found a problem in search of an answer, even if you stumble upon it. Never forget, you must work to meet market needs, not try to force fit your needs into the market.

CHAPTER 18

Business Battlefield Survival

If You Can't Change the Emotional Facts, Use Them!

Since we cannot alter other people's emotional idiosyncrasies or short-comings, sometimes, the best we can hope for is to use their eccentricities or blind spots to our advantage. Playing on emotional or psychological weakness to get what you need might sound too much like distasteful manipulation. Unfortunately, in business nothing is unfair when you're trying to deal with those whose behavior interferes with your livelihood, turning business into a no-holds-barred game of survival.

Hoping that you can deal with difficult or emotionally challenging individuals by reasoning with them is a fool's errand and believing there's a hope that they will respond to you fairly is utter foolishness. If you find this fact troubling, you're right! But that's the way it is. So, when all else fails, and you cannot end-run interference, you must play on the emotions and leverage the psychology of whoever is blocking you, in order to get what you need. Subtlety at first, but more directly if all else fails. Otherwise be prepared to lose.

We all, from time to time, use manipulative behavior that we judge acceptable. We do this without a second thought, bringing forward manipulative techniques we learned in childhood. Do you remember being taught as a child that lying was wrong and then watching the adults around you tell lies? If you asked why they lied, they probably explained the "little white lie" theory—that it's okay to lie to avoid hurting someone's feelings.

Maybe this explanation was confusing, but over time, you engaged in a little white lying to avoid uncomfortable situations, or to put others at ease. As people grow into adulthood, the little white lie rationalization expands to include bigger lies and manipulations.

It is no different in the world of business. People refine childhood behaviors to get what they need. The lawyer often gets an account by playing on the client's fears or anxieties. Effective salespeople frequently sell based on FUD—fear, uncertainty, and doubt. And the whole discipline of marketing is based on understanding customers' unattainable wants and needs and convincing them a product will deliver the impossible.

The most profitable consumer products are those which successfully convince buyers that they can help them lose weight, grow hair, look younger, find love and happiness, or make money the easy way. Barely any come close to working as promised, but marketers continue to exploit the consumer's persistent need to try new offers, hoping one will eventually delivers on its claims; the triumph of optimism over experience.

Aside from leveraging fear and insecurity, we can also get the results we seek with positive reinforcement: An insecure worker might lack confidence and believe they cannot achieve a set goal. A good manager or partner works around this, by providing encouragement and instilling confidence the employee lacks. A good coach bypasses a colleague's self-doubt and negative self-talk, replacing it with encouragement or affirmations. It's a benign form of manipulation.

We're not suggesting that you manipulate others indiscriminately by playing on their emotional weak points without discretion, because that's clearly unethical and will invariably come back to haunt you. But if all else fails and the choice is between constructively moving forward or not, you have to be ready to do whatever is necessary to safeguard your interests. If you allow yourself to be bulldozed by another's runaway emotions, insecurities, or problems, you are participating in your own destruction.

BEQ Case Study: Feigning Anger to Get a Bargain

Under the right circumstances, feigning anger, which is a form of manipulation, is a way for savvy businesspeople to get others to meet their needs. When an attorney, Henry, was approached by Paul, a long-standing client and an astute businessman, to help negotiate a contract, Paul requested that Henry cap his service fees at $20,000. Paul was adamant that he did not want the lion's share of his profit on the deal to be eaten up by runaway legal costs.

Henry was sympathetic. But explained that while he was keen to do the work for Paul, he feared that his firm might lose money on the project, because the time spent could easily exceed the proposed $20,000 fee. He suggested that they begin work, and that he would alert Paul, as they approached the $20,000 cap, and try to manage the time to avoid or minimize losses. Paul became irritated. "I think you're missing a point," he said. "I paid you over $200,000 in legal business last year. I'm disappointed that you won't share some risk on this deal, when I rarely ask you to do this."

Henry tried to smooth over Paul's irritation. "We appreciate your business," he said, "but we can't afford to run the business at a loss." Paul was now openly annoyed as he chastised Henry: "That's exactly my point. I can't afford to run my business at a loss, and squander the limited profit on a deal I've worked hard to close, due to exorbitant legal fees. You lawyers are all the same. You're unwilling to take risk, and always getting someone else to eat it all. How about you step up and have some skin in the game?"

Henry was perturbed. Paul was a good client and he did not want to kiss his business goodbye. "I'm not trying to be difficult," he said. "I have to be fair and act in the best interests of the firm." But this only increased Paul's apparent agitation. "What about being fair to me? Why should I keep giving you business and spending a fortune here, when you are unwilling to stick your neck out a little to help me on deals that have a narrow profit margin?" Henry relented: "Okay, okay, okay, don't get so bent out of shape. We'll cap the fees at $20,000."

The pair shook hands and Paul left satisfied. He had budgeted $25,000 for legal fees, but had tried feigning anger and squeezing Henry to knock the fee down. Paul knew that Henry needed the revenue, and was fearful of rocking the boat and losing the account. Paul would go on to use the same ploy periodically to save money on his legal bills. He didn't feel bad about it. Henry was making decent money on his business. Paul also knew that Henry was a little insecure about his ability as a lawyer. He wasn't sure enough of himself to call Paul's bluff and refuse to cap costs.

What Henry didn't realize was that Paul was highly satisfied with him as his legal counsel and had no intention of taking his business elsewhere. He would probably have paid full boat for the legal work if Henry had stuck to his guns and demanded it. Paul was willing to manipulate the situation to conserve cash that he needed for his business and to offset losses on bad deals. He was looking to save money wherever he could, and that included playing on Henry's insecurities.

Using Another's Anxiety

High BEQ players understand that taking advantage of another's anxiety can get the results they want. Telling an anxious businessperson not to be anxious seldom works, but knowing how to trigger another's anxiety to suit your purposes can pay off.

Remember we asked you earlier to be aware of advisors who point out problems with deals or business situation to trigger worry and undermine you? Here is where the script gets flipped. If you want to dissuade a colleague, associate, or partner from making a specific move, just point out concerns that you know will provoke their anxiety, so that you can steer them in the direction you think is best and works for you.

BEQ Case Study: Triggering Worry

Here's an excerpt from a Board of Directors meeting with the names changed to show you how this works. Peter and John were shareholders in a company called COREX Corporation. Peter, a chronic worrier, was discussing with John whether to pursue a merger with another company. The conversation went something like this:

Peter: I think we should pursue the merger with the CORX Corporation.

John: Peter, I'm not sure it's a good idea. How much do we know about the market for their product?

Peter: Enough to know, based on our due diligence, that there could be risk, but the company's earnings seem to be excellent. I'm sure the company's management knows what they are doing.

John: Are you saying that we will have to rely almost exclusively on the company's existing management?

Peter: I don't think we have a choice if we are to go forward, and I think that we should.

John: Peter, I think there could be execution risk with the current management team. I'd like you to take responsibility for researching and confirming that the COREX team is competent enough to justify the merger? If you think they can hold the earnings at the level they show this year, I will go along with it.

Peter: Well, I'm not sure I am qualified or comfortable in making that determination.

John: Peter, I am not suggesting that you make the determination, I'm merely suggesting that you take the responsibility for the outcome.

Peter: Let me think about it and I'll talk to you about it tomorrow.

John clearly knew that by putting responsibility for the outcome of the merger decision squarely on Peter, he would become anxious. And, as it turns out, John was correct. Peter came in the next day and suggested they pass on the merger.

Use Poor Market Conditions to Your Advantage

It's routine for professionals to proclaim that problems they're facing are caused by conditions beyond their control. How many times have you heard a company sales executive say that revenue is lagging due to the poor economy? This may be true, at least in part. The problem is that when the economy is bad, too many use it as an excuse to slack off, or give up putting forth focused effort until they receive reassurance that market conditions are once again picking up.

Once a negative atmosphere begins to descend on a business environment, people invariably become discouraged and even immobilized. However, the businessperson who refuses to buy into the ready excuse of not trying because of poor economic factors gains a competitive edge.

Inevitably, when people put in less effort because they are convinced conditions are bad and results will be poor, they are creating a space for more optimistic players to rush in and seize opportunities that still exist. These are often counterintuitive attitudes. Moving a company forward in a bad market definitely takes strong leadership, inspired thinking, and motivated performers.

But opportunities can be found regardless of conditions, if you don't succumb to the weak or pessimistic opinions of the slackers and naysayers. A seeming obstacle is often no more than a lighthouse directing you away from troubled waters. A high interest rate economy may curtail certain investments in residential construction, for example, while opening opportunities to invest in a business such as equipment leasing, which is not as hampered by interest rates. A dynamic marketplace, governed by a process of creative destruction, means that as some businesses fall, conditions are created for others to rise.

CHAPTER 19

Building a Personal Emotional Brand For Success

The Personal Brand Concept

The general focus of Marketing is to gain insight into what customers value and desire, in order to develop products and services that satisfy a target market, with the features, benefits, and experiences customers seek. Next, marketing uses branding and promotion to communicate relevant value to prospective buyers to maximize sales, profit, and loyalty.

Beyond the branding of products and services, much has been written about the personal brand—when professionals cultivate a reputation for delivering certain qualities and results, or a unique style or experience. Starting in the late 1990s, rapid tech innovation and market forces transformed the shape of work and the workplace. Professionals understood that they could no longer expect to be employed for decades by just one or two companies, until they eventually retired with a proverbial gold watch.

Global commerce and tech-inspired entrepreneurship have combined to make both the marketplace and the organizations that serve it more dynamic. The opportunities to launch a business, or to build skills and track record by jumping from company to company, have increased. Professionals now see themselves as valuable commodities to be packaged, branded and promoted in the marketplace for maximum distinction and gain.

The idea and commitment to developing a personal brand has become popular, as a way for professionals to communicate their unique value to an employer, organization, or investor. Within the marketing discipline, a brand is often defined not simply as the product itself, but how customers experience it. The brand is the positive or negative feelings and associations that it stimulates in customers. Personal branding follows similar lines.

Professionals with high Business EQ understand the value of shaping how others experience them in a business setting. This requires a clear understanding of the emotions and dynamics at play in business relationships and situations. The higher professionals seek to ascend in business, the more they must learn to manage their own emotions, as well as the feelings and impressions of those in their environment.

Some professionals cultivate a reputation for being ruthless or winning at all costs— "real killers". Companies bring them in to help negotiate high-stakes deals, to make painful organizational changes, to reverse a negative trend, or to shake up a culture that has become too stagnant. There's a breed of business professionals who are naturally and temperamentally suited for such a hard-nosed role. They are bottom-line and mission focused, and less concerned about the casualties of their merciless decisions. "There is no sentiment in business," they say, "I am paid to get results."

Others find themselves in the role of sacrificing employees and relationships for business objectives, but have a harder time reconciling themselves to outcomes. They may have to make tough decisions, but they far from relish it. In either case, central to the personal brand of each of these types is not allowing personal angst to get in the way of needed action.

Other leaders brand themselves as the coach of an all-star team. They are skilled in placing the perfect players in essential roles, building team spirit, and running a playbook that is geared to winning the business game.

Still other executives pride themselves on building productive and harmonious business cultures that minimize friction and destructive rivalry, and where teams feel part of a well-structured and emotionally stable community. They are content to make their contributions in service of excellence and for the good of the whole.

The speed of the team is the speed of the leader. Brilliant leaders can motivate a team to achieve inspired performance. Managers and professionals with strong Business EQ succeed in building personal brands, which run the gamut of talent that the marketplace seeks. Some are immensely creative, or necessarily disruptive, or ground-breaking, or contrarian. Others are amazing mentors, or act as a stabilizing force or steady hand. Each comes with a specific emotional fingerprint or sought-after style.

In thinking about your personal brand, take into consideration your emotional makeup. Do you like nurturing others? Building culture or organization? Being a star performer? Working alone? Do you play well with others, or find yourself intolerant when asked to manage the needs of others? Do you like being in the spotlight or behind the scenes? Your temperament and style are every bit as important as your functional skillset, knowledge, and capabilities.

Professionals often fail, not because they are incompetent and lack skills, but because they pursue roles that bring emotional challenges that they are not suited for or cannot accommodate, which creates resistance and drains their energy. High Business EQ professionals do not push the river. They don't try to swim against emotional currents and limitations that hold them back and drag them down. They let the current of their practical and emotional strengths carry them along to success.

Leaders often pursue training and development that enable them to manage the maximum number of people and situations with the greatest span of control. But it is the rare person who does not find personal fault lines—situations, colleagues or adversaries that throw them off balance and get the better of them.

Getting results and summiting in your career means respecting limitations, especially emotional limitations, yours and others. Both men and women often chase lofty career goals, but they still seek work and family balance. A percentage of people are so driven that they gladly sacrifice family to be happy workaholics. These all-or-nothing types won't look kindly on you if you are someone who knocks off at 5pm to catch your child's little league game. Alternatively, more casual but still ambitious players understand that it is possible to get spectacular results, without having to sacrifice all life outside of work, by putting in insanely long and often unproductive hours, which can lead to burn-out.

BEQ Case Studies: Judged on Results

Maggie was a financial professional who was results oriented and worked off hours to get the job done, so that she could fulfill important roles in her family and community. She had a quirky schedule and demanded time off for family and outside commitments. This cost her a number of jobs for violating "personal day" policies. Eventually, Maggie learned to make it clear to hiring managers that she wanted to be judged on performance and not on face time: "Give me goals, tell me what you want and leave me to do it. Don't look over my shoulder and manage my time."

This type of approach is best suited in companies where leadership supports self-starters in fostering a culture of personal accountability, rather than rigid rules and strict time keeping.

Seeking a Broader Span of Control

Bill handed in his resignation as head of sales operations, just one year after a large corporation acquired the cyber security firm, where he had spent five years on a team that had grown it from a start-up to a major competitor in the space, and a prime acquisition target. The acquiring company wanted to keep Bill, but he knew it was time to move on. "I used to be responsible for managing the whole pizza pie, and now I control only a tiny sliver of a slice," he said.

Bill realized that he loved the fast-pace and large span of control that came with working at start-ups, where every day was filled with challenges that stretched him and demanded ingenuity to meet them. Bill soon developed a strong reputational brand as the start-up guy you hire to build a first-rate sales operation from scratch.

Resisting Growth and Progress

Don hired his sister-in-law, Eileen, as bookkeeper when he started his manufacturing business. Five years later, Eileen was in over her head, unable to put into place the systems and software that the company needed to keep pace with growth. Don hired a new CFO, Simon, who laid down the law during his interviews for the position. "I have no interest in joining a sleepy mom-and-pop with a stagnant eight million dollars in annual sales," Simon said. "I am here to help you grow, and I expect people to get on board with the mission."

Don had hoped that Eileen would embrace the challenge to grow her business acumen under Simon's leadership, but instead she simply saw Simon as a disruptive threat, who wanted to undo her hard work, and had no appreciation for the 12-hour days she had put in to help Don's once fledgling company survive through its turbulent early days. She didn't want to be, but Eileen suddenly found herself being critical, divisive and disruptive. Defending "the way we do things around here" was more important to her than growing the business and adopting new practices, as Don and Simon now desired.

After six months, Eileen was forced reluctantly to admit that, despite her best efforts, she could not get on board with Simon's reorganization efforts in the finance department. Every change, new piece of software, and updated protocol felt like a slap in the face, instead of the progress it actually represented. She knew it was time to go. Emotionally, she could not adjust. Eileen liked small. Preferred mom and pop. Her calling, she realized, was working with start-ups to establish sound, basic bookkeeping practices.

Horses for Courses

Inventors and founders understand well the challenges of innovating a new product or service, but often are not the people to manage and grow a company once their product takes off. Accomplished managers understand that as a company begins to scale, process becomes more important than personalities. Pretty soon, it is no longer prudent to manage operations based only on what the boss and a small cohort think is the right way to go. Expert analysis and effective consensus building must come into play.

Often a founder finds it difficult to give up control, like a stubborn King Lear who cannot relinquish his kingdom to the next generation. At such times, a savvy board or outside investors will exert pressure to ensure a new type of leader is brought in, one who knows how to install solid operational structures and systems.

As companies are birthed, grow, mature and struggle for continued relevance in a fast-moving marketplace, fresh players with contrasting temperaments and emotional strengths are invited in to manage the transitions and ring important changes. And through every phase of development, a new emotional landscape emerges, demanding different talents to cultivate it. When circumstances shift, employees who once led the way find themselves sidelined, as new strengths are needed to meet emerging challenges:

- An executive who leads fast-paced growth is typically not the one who will be needed to stabilize operations.
- A founder who has won early customers through personal networking efforts is not the one to put in place professional marketing and sales, as a sleek engine to drive revenue.
- As a company moves through the milestones of its lifecycle, it will demand a different and changing cast of managers, who bring not only skills to meet the challenges at hand, but also the emotional intelligence to help move the culture and organization forward.

In leadership development, the concept of overusing a skill is well understood. We all have strengths. Lawyers, accountants, and many business operators, are known for being sensibly prudent, cautious and risk averse. These are valuable qualities except when they are ill-suited to the challenge.

One definition of a leader is the person who can make good decisions with only partial data. Business often demands savvy risk taking that can mean the difference between success and failure. The overly cautious manager is not the talent that is fitted to these circumstances.

The hammer seeks the nail is a popular phrase. It refers to people who cannot change their style to meet the challenge. They simply do what they know how to do best, whether it is appropriate or not. Slow and plodding does not work when nimble and fast are required. At other times, slow and steady is preferable to full-speed ahead.

Overuse of a skill means turning your talent into a liability, simply because it is too uncomfortable to acknowledge that an outlook, attitude, or talent, different than what you possess, is required. A high Business EQ professional is willing to be clear eyed about what is needed, set ego aside, and bring in the talent suited to meet the challenge at hand.

Determining Your BEQ Brand

Invest time to understand your emotional strengths and limitations:

- If you prefer emotional openness and honesty, it is not wise to work in companies, where feelings and communication are handled in a covert or restrained fashion.
- If you are a self-starter, who bridles at being suffocated by over supervision, don't opt for a manager who is a control freak.
- If you are a people whisperer, someone who knows how to diffuse difficult situations, head off conflict, and put others at their ease, seek out situations where your emotional strength is appreciated and rewarded, versus an environment where coworkers and bosses are closed to informal sharing and problem solving.

Every company and person possesses unique equity—qualities and talent configurations that are distinctive and particular to them. Aside from your professional resume, you also own emotional equity that is special to you—your emotional brand, as it were. You bring specific emotional strengths to the table. Maybe you are calm under fire; circumspect and discreet; outspoken, or the truth teller who is needed to shake things up. What's your emotional brand? Take time to figure it out and leverage it. Go where your emotional intelligence and temperament are celebrated and not criticized.

CHAPTER 20

The Wrap-Up

Key Elements of the Process

The process of change can be summarized by three A's: awareness, acceptance, and action. Strengthening BEQ is no different. First, you must become *aware* to what extent business, not unlike the rest of life, runs on emotions—those that are easily apparent and others that are hidden. Emotions that are productive and aid cohesion and progress, and others that hijack or trip us up.

Once *aware* of this reality, you must then overcome any cognitive dissonance, skepticism, or confusion, until you can *accept* it as fact. Next, it's time to take *action*, by making it a priority to decipher the emotional dynamics at play in any work situation. And then to develop effective strategies and take meaningful action to counter them.

As difficult as this can be, it is preferable to being continually blind-sided by emotional forces or undercurrents that you are unable to detect, because you have not recognized and factored in the powerful role that emotions play, whenever people come together to compete for business, professional, or career loss or gain.

In a Nutshell

Beyond the three As of awareness, acceptance, and action, let's summarize the key insights that those with high BEQ typically maintain, which we have shared in the book:

1. Business Is a Game

Game theorists and sociologists explain that most human and societal interactions, at both a macro and micro level, and at a personal and impersonal level, operate as a game of sorts. The game is governed by familiar rules, logic, role-playing, and repeating patterns of conduct that participants are trained or socialized into acting out—often unconsciously.

Savvy, street-smart, and high BEQ professionals are better able to see the game-like nature of business and view it more impersonally. They know that within the game of life, business is its own game. It is played out and repeated in a combination of new and familiar ways, demanding that participants adopt variations on established roles. Each game requires role-playing, solid strategy, and expert tactics to accomplish the objectives set forth.

Always remembering that business is a game helps us to step back, discern the rules, the players, and the action, and to understand which role we ourselves are adopting and playing—intentionally or otherwise. Failure to remember this means we often project our expectations, assumptions, misplaced emotions, or fantasies onto a work situation, winding up baffled when events don't play out, or associates fail to perform, as we anticipate or predict.

Not taking too personally the business game and how it unfolds, as well as the emotions that are acted out, is critical. Of course this is a tall order. We have spent an entire book explaining how personal emotional agendas override the impersonal nature of business, until it becomes a theater where psychodramas are enacted, regardless of how much we are told otherwise.

2. Negativity Is a Killer

As we have said repeatedly, negativity in all its forms undermines progress. Negative self-talk, self-doubt, or lack of confidence are unhelpful. Negative bosses, partners, associates, or subordinates are hinderances. Job number one is always spotting negativity in yourself and in your environment, and then eliminating or end running it. Endlessly second guessing, anticipating failure, seeking out criticism, or talking ourselves and others out of viable action, and into self-sabotage, signals negativity.

3. Staying Present Is Essential

We discussed the importance of developing and using plans as guideposts to get us moving forward with clear intention. But plans are not a promise of future profit or success written in stone. While we set out in a clear direction, it is essential that we stay grounded in the present, not getting too far ahead of the actual action.

Move confidently from A to B and forget Z for now—you can't get there from here. Avoid worrying and prognosticating, closing down options because you're convinced they won't pan out, or giving up based solely on inner doubt or worry.

Instead of not applying for a job, seeking a specific opportunity, or pursuing a cherished goal, because you tell yourself it will never happen, bravely take action and see what unfolds. Keep an eye on the future, but stay in the now, dealing with present realities instead of future imaginings.

4. Hone Your BEQ Skills as a Priority

Go into every new as well as familiar situation with your eyes wide open, ready and willing to read the emotional landscape, the people, and the emotional dynamics you encounter. You cannot act effectively until you have the emotional gist of things. Read the room and take appropriate actions to manage people and underlying agendas. Heading off problems and maintaining forward movement demands that you become a student of human nature and demonstrate BEQ at every turn.

5. Look for Patterns

Everyone is unique, but depending on their emotional makeup or unconscious emotional drives, people often act out their emotions, especially hidden ones, in similar ways. Revisit and keep building on the catalogue of clues we began that tip you off about what emotional undercurrents are present. And keep adding to the inventory of "emotional types or personalities" that we reviewed.

Over time, you will run again and again into the same or similar personality types in business, who drop the same or similar clues as to what their emotional motivations are. You will no longer be baffled by seemingly inexplicable or counterproductive behavior. Instead, you'll be increasingly confident about how to handle people and situations so they don't get in your way. Pretty soon, you'll see them coming and head them off before they have a chance to put a dint in your progress.

6. Know Thyself

An emotionally intelligent professional has taken a full inventory of personal strengths and limitations, including emotional blind spots or weaknesses. We recognize that there are traits or aspects of our emotional makeup that we can correct—some immediately, some over time. Other traits we may never overcome and they will, if we are not careful, continue to trip us up.

What's important is a continual process of self-examination and learning, so that we come to know ourselves better and better. We acknowledge which people, circumstances, and dynamics trigger us into acting out unproductively, as well as which scenarios and challenges arouse our strengths. Acting out of self-knowledge, with emotional maturity, is a hallmark of high BEQ.

7. Nothing to Fear But Fear Itself

No one is denying that managing ourselves and others in the workplace is serious even scary business: our survival, security, reputation, happiness, and future can depend on it. Progress is hampered, however, when we allow ourselves to mistake feelings for facts, and be driven by emotions, especially chronic fear, uncertainty, and worry.

Ignoring emotions is certainly not the point. We've spent the entire book trying to wake readers up to taking emotion in business seriously, by recognizing the impacts it creates. It's by identifying the emotions at play that we confront them head on and diffuse the unproductive ones.

It's when emotion operates beneath the surface or outside of our awareness that it entraps us or trips us up. Recognizing emotion for what it is, and putting it in its place, makes it far easier to break a problem down and apply logic to solve it. In this way we stop ourselves from being gripped by irrational feelings that can keep us stuck for years.

8. Friendly, Not Friends

We can enjoy close working relationship with colleagues and associates. And people who work together certainly can and do become friends, especially after many years of close and productive association. However, as we explored, it's a mistake to go into our business or work life primarily in search of friends or a surrogate family. And if we do, we must be clear about the extent to which we do this, and the trade-offs or problems it creates.

It is said that in life one expectation is too many. Assuming or expecting that people and situations will not disappoint us sets us up for disaster. Of course, people and circumstance often satisfy and delight us, but it's a mistake to take this for granted. This is especially true in business. Your workmates may function as family, but they are not. Keep a clear, bright line between work and personal relationships, and manage needs and expectations accordingly.

Setting Effective Goals for Profit by Recognizing Reality

Using repetition and denial, society and business culture have convinced us that having emotional difficulties at work is something to be ashamed of or embarrassed about. That's why we often deny the emotions at play in ourselves and others, for fear something might be wrong with us or unacceptable.

Think back to a moment when someone at work suggested that you were being emotional in response to a situation. Did you readily agree and calmly say that you would look into it and get to the bottom of your reaction? If so, you're pretty secure, emotionally mature even. Too many tend to become defensive and deny being emotional.

Here's your formula to ensure that you're on the right track in increasing your emotional awareness:

1. Acknowledge the possibility that emotional issues of all kinds sabotage the business environment—they could be yours or those of the people you're working with, or both.
2. Learn to recognize clues to the existence of emotional roadblocks.
3. Accept any destructive emotional issues that you cannot eliminate.
4. Know that if you do not accept and work to change your own emotionally destructive issues, you will be controlled by them.
5. Accept that if you cannot change an emotional roadblock—either yours or those of others—you must and can work around it.

6. Recognize that if someone's emotional issues are blocking your progress, getting angry or otherwise acting out your frustration won't do any good. You must create a situation which causes him to go in your direction or frees you to sprint past him.

7. Accept that people who do not recognize their own emotional roadblocks are easily led astray. And don't put yourself in that spot.

8. Identify the circumstances and work through all your thoughts and feelings when you think emotional factors may be involved in a business situation.

9. Be open to the fact that in the early stages of your awareness development, it will help speed your progress if you put all of this in writing in your Development Diary.

10. Develop a strategy to move you forward, something that, in each situation, will be clear once your see the roadblock issues.

What to Expect

As you begin increasing your emotional awareness, expect to experience bouts of anxiety followed by periods of exhaustion, even disorientation—all seemingly out of nowhere, for no particular reason, and not from any source you can identify. You may also have moments when you feel as if you've failed in life or in business, and feel too discouraged to go on.

You might even fear losing everything, as you're beset by negative and self-defeating thoughts. As these thoughts and feelings surface, keep them right in front of you, shining a light of awareness on them. Track them in your Development Diary, so you can revisit them later.

Where do these disruptive thoughts and feelings come from? They often arise as a result of our challenging previously ingrained conditioning—the too many years we spent blindly following received opinions, misplaced advice, or unhelpful beliefs that no longer fit current circumstances or goals—assuming they ever did.

Over time, these preconditioned beliefs manifest as an unconscious self or subpersonality that uses misleading self-talk and irrational feeling states to control us. Challenging this conditioned self with new emotional awareness creates turmoil, as we struggle to break the status quo and move out of our old emotional comfort zone.

If we persevere, however, we can move forward under our authentic power, using new insight, making sense of the world as we go, and acting out of confidence and a belief that we can stay the business course and make it work.

Above all, know that you can push through any emotional discomfort and eventually get to the other side. There may be a few sleepless nights, but sooner than you think, there will be emotional sunshine. And success. Recognize that the very reason you're experiencing anxiety or discomfort is that you are now, finally, becoming unstuck and progressing, even though from your vantage point this may not be apparent.

You're Ready

You now have powerful new business awareness tools for understanding yourself and others, and how you and they operate emotionally in the business environment. Using these tools, and your growing BEQ, will enable you to quickly see when you're drifting, or in fact rushing, down the wrong path—when unproductive emotional agendas are hampering or totally blocking your ability to achieve your full potential in business, as well as in life.

The key to progress is to always be alert to what is happening emotionally. Your ability to identify and work with emotional roadblocks will improve as you acknowledge their presence. As you do, your progress will accelerate. Hold on to your hat. And good luck!

About the Authors

Richard M. Contino, Esq. is an internationally recognized entrepreneur, attorney, businessman, and negotiator. He has undertaken hundreds of high-stakes business, financial, and legal negotiations—aiding clients, companies, and partners in navigating complex power dynamics to forge multimillion dollar agreements and cross a business finish line. He is a Managing Director of First Lease Advisors and Captive Lease Advisors, equipment leasing and financing consulting firms; a Managing Director of Fairfield Capital Group, LLC, an equipment lease syndication firm and the Managing Partner of Contino + Partners, a law firm whose practice is limited to equipment leasing and financing. He has an LL.M. (Corporate Law) from the New York University Graduate School of Law; a Juris Doctor from the University of Maryland School of Law, and a Bachelor of Aeronautical Engineering from Rensselaer Polytechnic Institute. He is a member of the Bar of the State of New York and has been admitted to the Bars in State of Maryland and District of Columbia. Contino is also a member of the American and New York State Bar Associations, and is listed in Who's Who of American Law, Who's Who of Emerging Leaders, Who's Who in the World, and The International Who's Who of Contemporary Achievement.

Penelope J. Holt is a marketing, advertising, and communications executive and consultant. She has worked with and for numerous leading companies, including PayPal, eBay, Pitney Bowes, British Telecom, American Management Association, Sumitomo Mitsui Banking Corp, as well as with notable startups in the technology, fintech, ecommerce, and credit space. As a communications specialist and writer, she has collaborated with business thought leaders and influencers to bring their ideas to market through innumerable books, speeches, articles, and compelling business content. She holds joint honors degrees in linguistics and English literature from York University, England, where she was born and educated. She is married and a mother of two, and lives in New York.

Index

OTHER TITLES IN THE BUSINESS CAREER DEVELOPMENT COLLECTION

Vilma Barr, Consultant, Editor

- *Finding Your Career Niche* by Anne S. Klein
- *Shaping Your Future* by Rita Rocker-Craft
- *The Trust Factor* by Russell von Frank
- *Financing New Ventures* by Geoffrey Gregson
- *Strategic Bootstrapping* by Matthew W. Rutherford
- *Creating A Business and Personal Legacy* by Mark J. Munoz
- *Innovative Selling* by Eden White
- *Present! Connect!* by Tom Guggino
- *Introduction to Business* by Patrice Flynn
- *Be Different!* by Stan Silverman

Announcing the Business Expert Press Digital Library

Concise e-books business students need for classroom and research

This book can also be purchased in an e-book collection by your library as

- a one-time purchase,
- that is owned forever,
- allows for simultaneous readers,
- has no restrictions on printing, and
- can be downloaded as PDFs from within the library community.

Our digital library collections are a great solution to beat the rising cost of textbooks. E-books can be loaded into their course management systems or onto students' e-book readers.
The **Business Expert Press** digital libraries are very affordable, with no obligation to buy in future years. For more information, please visit **www.businessexpertpress.com/librarians**. To set up a trial in the United States, please email **sales@businessexpertpress.com**.